The Witchcraft Almanac

The Witchcraft Almanac

Seasonal spells & magical rituals for every day of the year

Midia Star

GODSFIELD

First published in Great Britain in 2026 by Godsfield,
an imprint of Octopus Publishing Group Ltd
Carmelite House
50 Victoria Embankment
London EC4Y 0DZ
www.octopusbooks.co.uk

An Hachette UK Company
www.hachette.co.uk

The authorized representative in the EEA is Hachette Ireland, 8 Castlecourt Centre, Dublin 15, D15 XTP3, Ireland (email: info@hbgi.ie)

Distributed in the US by Hachette Book Group
1290 Avenue of the Americas, 4th and 5th Floors
New York, NY 10104

Distributed in Canada by Canadian Manda Group
664 Annette St., Toronto, Ontario, Canada M6S 2C8

ISBN: 978 1 84181 649 4
eISBN: 978 1 84181 650 0

A CIP catalogue record for this book is available from the British Library.

MIX
Paper | Supporting responsible forestry
FSC® C008047

Printed and bound in China.

10 9 8 7 6 5 4 3 2 1

Commissioning Editor: Louisa Johnson
Assistant Editor: Alice Gawthrop
Copyeditor: Tara O'Sullivan
Art Director: Yasia Williams
Illustrator: Coni Curi
Picture Manager: Jennifer Veall
Production Manager: Allison Gonsalves

Disclaimer: Any application of the ideas and information contained in this book is at the reader's sole discretion and risk.

Use caution when using essential oils on the skin as they may cause irritation. People with sensitivities or allergies should avoid use.

Neither Octopus Publishing Group Ltd or the author take any responsibility for any individual reaction to any particular ingredient, or any consequences resulting from the use of information contained in this book.

Additional Picture Credits:
iStock: elenabs 143, JuliarStudio 113, Serhii Borodin 79, 117, 127, Veronika Oliinyk 139, zager 124

CONTENTS

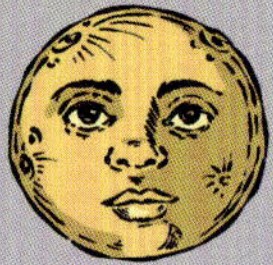

INTRODUCTION

Welcome to your year of magic

This book is a companion for your journey through the seasons, offering a way to live more closely in rhythm with nature and to bring a little magic into each day. Within these pages, you'll find 365 spells, along with guidance on the festivals of the Pagan calendar, the shifting energies of each season and the simple tools that help focus intention.

Think of this book as part almanac and part spellbook. It is not about rigid rules or secret knowledge, but rather about connection: to yourself, to the earth and to the turning of the seasons. While there is a spell for every day of the year, this almanac is designed so that you can follow it during any calendar year. The spells are thematic for the month rather than being tied to a specific date, allowing you to weave them into your practice in a way that feels intuitive.

Each section of the book begins with the start of a new season: winter, spring, summer and autumn. In each season's opening pages, you'll discover the qualities of that time of year, the Sabbats celebrated within it, and the ingredients nature offers most readily at this time. This book was written with the Northern Hemisphere in mind, so you may wish to adjust some aspects, such as seasonal dates or ingredients, depending on where you are in the world.

The spells that follow are grouped into smaller subsections. Each spell section typically begins with magic to support the seasonal transition, moves into spells tied to specific seasonal celebrations and concludes with spells to prepare you for the next cycle. Additionally, every spell is coded for easy reference, so you can quickly find what you need, whether it's a love spell, a protection charm or a spell for personal growth. Some spells are drawn from centuries-old traditions and others are adjusted to suit modern life.

You'll find that several spells also call upon seasonal deities from all over the world to enhance their power. Witches call upon many gods and goddesses from different religions and cultures, believing that at the heart, we are all one.

Above all, this book is here to help you find your own way. You don't need rare herbs or expensive tools; your most powerful ingredient is always your intention. Every spell can be adjusted to suit your life, your environment, your energy and your curiosity.

Wherever you are on your path – beginner, lifelong witch or just curious – this almanac is here to remind you that magic is not something outside of yourself. It is in the seasons, in the cycles, in the small rituals of daily life. Most of all, it is in you.

A brief history of witchcraft

Witchcraft is typically understood as a belief in magic, supernatural forces or spiritual energies. Witches draw upon the natural world and its powers to lead positive, authentic lives – not just for themselves, but often in service of others too. Despite its recent resurgence, being a witch or practising witchcraft still carries historical stigma in many cultures, often seen (incorrectly) as something dark, evil or dangerous.

It's widely believed that witchcraft has roots in ancient Pagan religions. The word 'Pagan' comes from the Latin *paganus*, meaning 'rural' or 'country-dweller'. It was originally used by early Christians as a dismissive term for those who followed older, nature-based spiritual practices. To them, anyone outside of Christianity was a non-believer, often viewed as uneducated or lesser.

The term 'paganism' was eventually reclaimed, becoming an umbrella term for a wide variety of spiritual paths that honour nature, the elements and ancient traditions. It has evolved into something to celebrate rather than suppress. Today, witchcraft is even considered pretty cool.

Wicca is the modern term for the Pagan religion, which encompasses the ancient practices of Paganism and the modern earth-centred religion. Practitioners of Wicca calls themselves Wiccans.

Witchcraft embraces many different elements from many different faiths, including Celtic, Nordic and Gaelic traditions, making it an ideal path for those who don't want a one-size-fits-all belief system. It offers space to explore and blend different cultural and magical practices. Most people who are drawn to witchcraft are unique, often found on the fringes of society. They're not afraid to ask questions or challenge norms.

The 'old ways' of the Wiccan and Pagan paths are constantly evolving, and nowadays these practices have become more accessible and intuitive. Gone are the rigid rules that say you must do things a certain way just because an old tome told you to. Witchcraft today is more about modifying spells to suit your life and focusing on what truly matters: your intention.

Whatever you wish to call it, practising witchcraft is about living in harmony with nature, honouring diversity and being true to yourself – and doing so with kindness and integrity, and without harming others. I define a 'witch' today as someone who dedicates themselves to lifelong learning about our connection to nature and all living things. Being a witch is a lifestyle, and a wonderful one at that.

There is nothing you cannot do when you learn the Craft; it will empower you and make you realize just how much control and influence you can have over your life.

The Wheel of the Year

In Wiccan/Pagan circles, while we do live our modern lives in accordance with the Gregorian calendar, we also take note of the Wheel of the Year, also known as the Pagan Calendar. The Wheel of the Year consists of eight seasonal festivals, known as the Wiccan Sabbats, that are celebrated throughout the year for their symbolic connection to the changing of the seasons.

The eight festivals are:

- **Winter Solstice** (Also known as Yule or Midwinter)
- **Imbolc** (Also known as Candlemas)
- **Ostara** (Also known as the Spring Equinox)
- **Beltane** (Also known as May Day)
- **Litha** (Also known as Midsummer)
- **Lughnasadh** (Also known as Lammas)
- **Mabon** (Also known as the Autumn Equinox)
- **Samhain** (Also known as All Hallows or Halloween)

It is widely believed that these festivals were celebrated all over ancient Europe, combining the four Celtic fire festivals with the Anglo-Saxon solstices and equinoxes.

The precise dates often vary depending on local traditions, climate and which hemisphere you live in. However, the meaning behind all the festivals is the same: to celebrate and give thanks to all that nature provides. As you make your way through this book you will learn about each of these celebrations in turn.

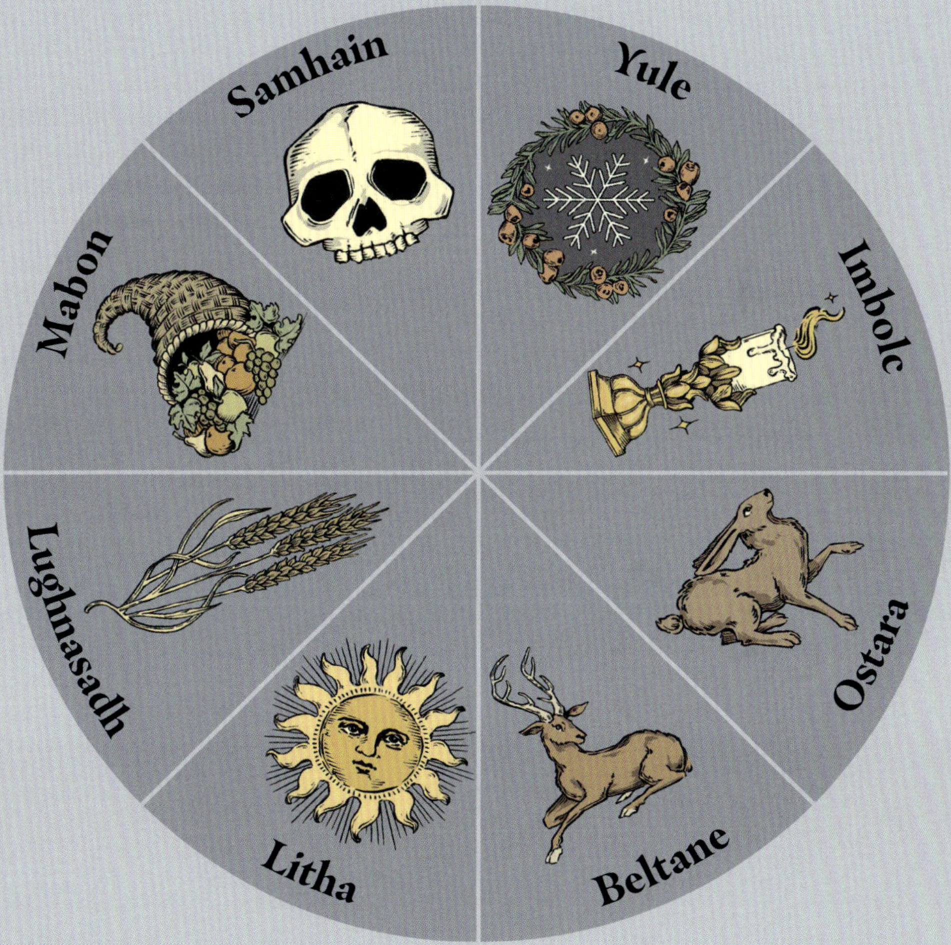
Samhain
Yule
Imbolc
Ostara
Beltane
Litha
Lughnasadh
Mabon

Lunar cycles

The moon holds great significance in a witch's practice. Its energy can be harnessed to support and enhance spellcasting. Each phase of the moon carries its own distinct energy, and while it's not always essential to cast spells according to a specific phase, aligning with the moon can amplify a spell's effectiveness and speed up its results.

The moon completes its orbit around the Earth roughly every 29.5 days, passing through eight phases: new moon, waxing crescent, first quarter, waxing gibbous, full moon, waning gibbous, third quarter and waning crescent.

Different types of spells are often best suited to particular moon phases, allowing witches to work with the moon's natural rhythm for optimal results.

Below are the four main moon phases I mention in this book, and the types of spells best suited to these parts of the lunar cycle.

- **New moon:** New beginnings, fresh starts, releasing the past, long-term goals, manifestations, new opportunities.
- **Waxing moon:** Wishes, growth, prosperity, luck, confidence, decision-making, empowerment, positive change.
- **Full moon:** Any spell – magic performed during the full moon is the most powerful of all magic.
- **Waning moon:** Banishment, purging, purifying, karma, justice, protection.

A note on spells

Remember: witchcraft is and always has been about intention – that's your most powerful tool. This book is here to empower you, offering guidance rather than rules. It's here to help you let go of outdated myths and start trusting your own intuition. With time and with practice, you'll learn just how strong your energy really is.

While each spell is designed to be cast during a particular season, that doesn't mean you must wait for a specific time of year. For instance, if you come across a winter spell that resonates with you in the middle of spring, go ahead and cast it. The magic will still work; you may just need to adjust the ingredients depending on what's available to you in the present moment.

The same flexibility applies to spell timing generally. If you can't wait for the recommended lunar phase or day of the week, go ahead and perform the spell regardless. While the day of the week, moon and planetary alignments can amplify your magic, they're not essential. If your intention is strong, your spell will still work.

If a spell calls for a specific herb, flower, crystal or other ingredient that you do not have, don't worry. You can substitute it with something similar, or with something that simply feels right to you. I've tried to make the ingredients and tools in this book as simple and accessible as possible, and where alternatives exist, I've suggested them. I always recommend keeping a few basics in your cupboard: white candles, a clear quartz crystal and salt. Even if you have nothing else, these three can carry you through just about any spell.

And don't sweat it if you make a mistake. There is no 'right' way to be a witch. If you do wish to 'undo' any spell, just take a deep breath, set the intention to cancel or restart the spell, and try again. Magic isn't about perfection, it's about connection.

Witchcraft is personal. Whether you work solo or in a coven, your path is your own. Take inspiration from others, but don't let anyone tell you there's only one 'true' way. The key is experiment, observe, learn and track what works for you. I recommend you keep a Book of Shadows – a personal journal of your spellwork. Write down what you used, how you felt, what substitutions you made and how long it took for results to show up. This is how witches have passed down knowledge for centuries, and how you'll build your own practice.

You are the magic, and there's nothing you can't do with a little intention, some self-belief and the will to make it happen. So, follow your curiosity and trust your own energy. This is your Craft.

Spell preparation & guiding principles

Before casting any spell, it's important to take a moment to protect and ground yourself and get yourself into the right mindset, because your energy influences the outcome of your magic.

Here are a few easy ways to do this:

- Draw a circle of salt around your space.
- Light a white tealight candle as a symbol of protection.
- Visualize a white light surrounding your body like a shield.

Whichever method you choose, make it part of your spellcasting ritual. Think of it as creating sacred space.

I only have a few 'rules' that I abide by as a witch:

- **Avoid casting more than one spell a day.** Casting too many spells in quick succession can dilute your focus and muddle your intentions. You must give each spell the time and space it needs to unfold.
- **Never cast a spell when you're angry or upset, especially if the spell involves another person.** Spells are all energy-based, and your energy is very powerful when you're angry. Magic cast in a negative state can backfire or ripple out in ways you didn't intend. Instead, trust in the universe. The laws of karma are real; any person who causes harm will eventually receive their punishment.

So, take a deep breath and ground yourself using the suggested methods before performing any magic.

A few basic safety notes

- **Health-focused spells should not be seen as a substitute for professional medical advice.** Always take care when working with naked flames, and make sure you place any candles or incense in a suitable holder. Use gloves when handling nettles or greenery that may have thorns, avoid ingredients to which you are allergic and always dispose of materials in the appropriate way. Do not drink nettle tea if you take blood thinners.

- **When foraging, never consume anything without being completely certain that it is safe to eat.** Gain permission before foraging from public or private land, and take only what you need.

- **Always take care when using essential oils.** If you are pregnant, breastfeeding, have a medical condition or are taking prescribed medication, consult with your healthcare provider before use. Avoid using essential oils on sensitive or broken skin. You can substitute essential oils with the relevant dried herb in any spell.

Now, let's get on with spellcasting!

Spell categories

- **Fortune & prosperity**
- **Home & cleansing**
- **Protection, purging & justice**
- **Love, family & relationships**
- **Healing & self-care**
- **Gratitude & manifesting**
- **Guidance & prophecy**
- **Success, change & transformation**
- **General spell practice**

WINTER

In the Wiccan calendar, winter is the time for deep rest and sleep. As nature takes a break and hibernates, we too are invited to slow down and turn inward. Now is the time to reflect on the past year and prepare for new beginnings. In most of Europe, the winter period runs from the end of November through to the end of February. Even if you live in a warmer climate, the energetic themes of winter remain the same: stillness, introspection, purification and renewal.

Winter festivals & celebrations

Winter Solstice

(Yule/Midwinter/Alban Arthan)

The Winter Solstice, which falls on or around 21 December, marks the longest night of winter before the return of the sun. In the Neo-Druidic tradition, drawn from Celtic roots, this turning point is known as Alban Arthan. Folklore tells us that Druids would gather beneath the oldest oak tree to cut sprigs of mistletoe, catching them before they touched the ground to ensure prosperity for the year ahead.

For witches, the Winter Solstice is a time to honour the gods and goddesses and the gifts of nature received over the past year, while also welcoming the rebirth of light and life. Traditions include decorating evergreen trees, burning Yule logs for good fortune and celebrating with feasts and offerings of gratitude. Many of these traditions pre-date Christianity and were later adopted and woven into Christmas practices.

Within this book, I will refer to the Winter Solstice and Yule interchangeably.

Imbolc *(Candlemas)*

Imbolc is the Gaelic festival that marks the first stirrings of spring. Traditionally celebrated in the first week of February (on 1 or 2 February), it is a time for clearing away the old and welcoming the new. As the earth begins to awaken, trees and plants prepare to bud and bloom for the year ahead.

The Celts and later Neo-Pagans honoured the goddess Brigid, patron of healing, smithing and poetry, by cleansing their homes of stagnant or negative energy. It was also believed that celebrating Imbolc ensured a successful harvest to come.

Imbolc is one of the greater Sabbats, or fire festivals, representing the return of light after the darkness of winter. Witches often mark the day with candles and bonfires, symbolizing the spark of new life.

Imbolc is a powerful time for renewal, cleansing and growth spells, especially those that sweep away what no longer serves you.

Winter goddesses

Beira ***(Cailleach or Queen of Winter)***
Beira is revered in Scottish folklore as a goddess of winter, creation and the rugged Scottish landscape. Often portrayed as a one-eyed crone, Beira wields the power to summon storms, carve mountains and herald the arrival of the winter season.

Skaði
In Norse mythology, Skaði is the goddess of winter, hunting and mountains. Fierce and independent, she embodies endurance and resilience. Her name is thought to derive from the Old Norse word *skaði*, which can be translated as 'harm', 'damage' or 'shadow'. Skaði is often invoked for strength during the hardest months, when survival depends on skill, patience and adaptability.

Chione
Chione is the Greek goddess of snow. A daughter of Boreas, the North Wind, she personifies the stillness and purity of snowfall. Chione reminds us that winter is harsh but also gentle, blanketing the earth in beauty and silence to prepare for rebirth.

Winter tips & recommendations

Ingredient access
Because winter can limit access to fresh herbs or flowers, the spells in this book are designed with availability in mind. Many ingredients can be found dried or substituted easily. I also recommend harvesting and drying fruits, seeds and herbs earlier in the year in preparation for winter. Readily available ingredients in colder months include mistletoe, holly, pansies, heather, poinsettias and fallen branches from bare trees. If you live in warmer climates, you can always substitute any unattainable ingredients with your local flora.

Observing nature
We often forget to admire the beauty of winter, so take walks to reconnect with nature. Winter is often called 'stick season' because in many countries, it strips everything back to reveal wood in its purest form. You may spot old bird nests, bare branches or mistletoe, each demonstrating nature's quiet resilience.

Crafting tools
This is an ideal time to collect naturally fallen branches for wand-making, broom-crafting or bonfires. Remember to always thank the tree and avoid cutting from living wood if possible.

Best spell types for winter
Spells centring protection, finances, celebration, introspection, healing, manifesting, love and self-love are especially powerful at this time of year.

WINTER SPELLS

Finance the festivities spell

The dark season often asks more of our purses, with gifts, feasts and gatherings to provide for. This spell helps ensure you have the resources you need to enjoy the season in comfort by calling on Lakshmi, the Hindu goddess of wealth, fortune and prosperity. For best results, cast on a Wednesday during a waxing moon at the start of December.

YOU WILL NEED *a magazine, scissors, glue, a sheet of paper, a pen, an envelope, a silver coin, a silver candle and matches.*

Look through the magazine and cut out pictures representing the things that you most want. This could be toys for any children in your life, gifts for friends or simply a little treat for yourself. Stick the images on to the sheet of paper and next to each one, write down why you want it. Is a particular item going to bring you joy? Are you looking forward to seeing the look on your child's face when they open the gift you've bought them? Fold the paper into three and place it in the envelope, along with the silver coin.

Light the silver candle and say the following three times:

'Goddess Lakshmi, hear my plea:
send this item on to me.
May I have the funds that I require
to buy this item and make me smile.'

Allow the candle to safely burn down and place the envelope under your pillow for the next seven nights. You will soon see an increase in prosperity.

Winter illness protection spell

The harsh weather can leave us feeling vulnerable. This charm shields you against both illness and unwanted energies. For best results, cast on a Sunday.

YOU WILL NEED *3 drops of lavender essential oil, 3 drops of peppermint essential oil, a white candle, a photo of yourself and matches.*

Rub the lavender oil and peppermint oil into the white candle, and allow the oil to seep into the wax for a few minutes. Place the candle securely into a candle holder, then place the photograph of yourself underneath. Repeat the following words three times:

'I am healthy and happy, and I create a magical boundary around myself for self-preservation during this harsh time. Nothing can penetrate this barrier. So mote it be.'

Allow the candle to safely burn down and put your photo back where it came from. You will now be protected from the winter season's coughs and colds, as well as any negative energy from the people you come into contact with.

Winter smoke stick

Smoke has been used for centuries to cleanse and refresh spaces. Craft a seasonal smoke stick to clear stagnant energies and welcome fresh energy.

YOU WILL NEED *some evergreen winter sprigs (such as pine, fir, cedar or holly), natural twine (not plastic or synthetic), scissors and matches.*

Go foraging in the woods for different evergreen sprigs. Even if it's a dry day, the sprigs will still have some moisture in them, so dry them in a warm space for 48 hours. Once dry, gather all your sprigs into a small bundle and cut off any loose ends. Secure your bundle with the twine.

Light the end of the bundle - it might crackle a little - then blow out any flames. Your bundle should now be producing natural smoke. If it doesn't, you may need to dry it out for a few more days.

Starting inside your front door, wave the smoke stick in the air. Pay attention to any corners where stagnant energy can remain stuck. Walk around your home and let the smoke drift into every room, repeating the following words:

'Bad or negative energy, you may go now, and only positive vibrations may come into my home.'

When you've cleansed every room, extinguish the smoke stick for use another time.

Comfort spell

When someone you care for is facing hardship in the dark of winter, this spell carries warmth to their spirit. Calling on Athena, Greek goddess of wisdom and warfare, it channels the steady glow of the hearth to offer comfort, care and strength.

YOU WILL NEED *silver biodegradable glitter, soft modelling clay, a bay leaf, a white tealight candle and matches.*

Place some silver glitter in your hands, then roll the modelling clay between them. As you do so, think about the troubles your friend or loved one is going through right now. Once your modelling clay is covered in glitter, gently create a little person out of the glittery clay. This is going to represent your friend or loved one.

Place your model on top of the bay leaf, then place the candle behind it. Light the candle and say:

'Goddess Athena, please help (name).
May you take on this problem as your own.
May you bring (name) comfort and healing,
and may their worries be gone
and their troubles be banished.
This is my request, so mote it be.'

Allow the candle to safely burn away and leave the clay figure on a windowsill that catches the winter sun. After 24 hours, dispose of the figure. The spell is now cast, and the person who needs help should soon report that things have improved.

Garlic money spell

This season of generosity can strain our reserves, but a simple garlic bulb can help replenish your funds, as garlic has been long honoured for its powers of prosperity. For best results, cast on a Friday.

YOU WILL NEED *the papery outer peel of 3 garlic bulbs, a fireproof dish and matches.*

Place the papery white peelings from the garlic bulb into a fireproof dish. Say the following words as you light the peelings and walk around your home with the dish, allowing the smoke to drift into the air:

'Money is returned to me, quickly and with ease. So mote it be.'

Make moon water

By charging water with the light of the moon, you can enhance the power of any water-based spell. You can make moon water at any time, but the energy is most potent during a full moon, when lunar power is at its peak.

YOU WILL NEED *a glass jar with a lid and some water.*

Simply fill your jar with water, place the lid on top of the jar and leave it outside for one night when the moon is at its fullest. Use the water in future spells.

Fruity luck garland

Citrus fruits are associated with purification, protection, abundance and prosperity. Craft this garland to draw good fortune into your home.

YOU WILL NEED *some natural string, dried orange and lemon slices and a knitting needle.*

To make this lovely lucky decoration, simply tie a knot in the end of a piece of string, then take a dried slice of orange, make a small hole in it with the knitting needle and thread it on to the string. Tie another knot, then repeat with a slice of lemon, then orange and so on, tying a knot between each one.

Hang this above your fireplace for luck during the winter season.

Winter wreath of protection

Creating a magical winter wreath invites protection and good fortune into your home during the dark months. This spell can be performed at any point in the season, using foraged greenery and natural treasures.

YOU WILL NEED *gardening gloves, several bare, pliable branches (such as willow), a large round bucket or bowl, garden twine, foraged items like pinecones and evergreen leaves (such as holly, heather and mistletoe), a glue gun and glue, blue ribbon, and photographs and personal items (optional).*

Wearing gardening gloves, bend and shape your branches around a large bucket or bowl, so that they form a circle. Secure the branches together with the garden twine until you have something that looks like the outer circle of a bird's nest.

Once you're happy that it will hold its shape, remove the bucket or bowl.

Add your foraged items, gluing on the pinecones and threading the leaves into the branches. Attach a loop of lucky blue ribbon at the top to hang the wreath. If you like, you can add photos or other personal items.

When you're happy with your wreath, hold it above your head and say:

'By the power of Skaði, the winter goddess, bless this home for the dark months cometh. With gratitude and intention, so mote it be.'

Your wreath is now blessed, and you can hang it on your front door.

Harmonious home spell

During the festive season, we welcome a lot of guests into our space, and some can bring in negative energy. This ritual restores balance to the home, sweeping away lingering tensions and inviting harmony. For best results, cast on a Thursday during a waxing-moon phase or just after visitors depart.

YOU WILL NEED *salt, a bowl, 1 teaspoon cinnamon, an onion, a knife, a blue candle, a white candle, a green candle and matches.*

Pour the salt into the bowl until it is halfway full. Add the cinnamon and mix. Cut the onion in half and press each half into the mixture. Light the candles in this order - blue (for calm), green (for prosperity) and white (for peace). Say the following words:

'Athena, warrior goddess of order and peace, hear my cry and take hold of this. Banish all negativity from my home, so that I feel calm and rested once again. Protect me and mine always. Bringing in peace, positive energy and healing to this home. So mote it be.'

While you wait for the candles to safely burn down, sprinkle the salt and cinnamon mixture in every room in your house. Leave the onion halves inside your home, placing one near the front door and the other near the back door.

Leave the onion halves in place for seven days.

Prosperity spell

Winter's pause invites reflection on work and goals. This spell opens the way toward growth and success. For best results, cast on a Thursday.

YOU WILL NEED *a red pen, 9 bay leaves, a bowl and salt.*

Use the red pen to write something associated with what you desire on each bay leaf. This could be the amount of money you need, or new clients for your business. Write something different on each leaf.

Fill a bowl with salt, then add the bay leaves to the bowl. Place the bowl in the furthest left corner of your home and leave it for 28 days.

Winter fragrance room freshener

Scent has the power to shift mood and energy. This fragrance charm refreshes stagnant spaces.

YOU WILL NEED *a hessian bag, cinnamon sticks, vanilla pods, dried orange slices, dried lemon slices, pine needles, a handful of cloves, a pinch of salt, water and a saucepan.*

Take the hessian bag and fill it with the cinnamon, vanilla, citrus slices, pine needles and cloves, adding a pinch of salt for luck. Close the bag. Fill a pan with water and place it over a low heat. Add the hessian bag to the pan and leave it to simmer and fill your home with fragrance. Keep an eye on the pan so that it doesn't boil dry.

Kinship peace spell

This spell soothes discord and encourages empathy within a household. For best results, cast during a waning-moon phase.

YOU WILL NEED *a tall white candle, 2 silver pins, a clear quartz crystal and matches.*

Push the first silver pin, which represents you, into the top half of the candle, then push the second pin, which represents the other person, about 5cm (2in) below it. Place the quartz crystal in front of the candle. Light the candle and say:

'The arguments will cease; the power of light will restore peace.'

Wait until the candle burns down enough that the first pin drops out of the candle, then say the following:

'Peace has been restored; bitterness is no more.'

Now wait until the second pin drops from the candle, then allow the candle to safely burn down. To finish the spell, carry your clear quartz with you for seven days and conceal the pins somewhere in your clothing.

Snow protection spell

If you're lucky enough to wake up to a blanket of snow, be grateful – nature has just blessed you with a powerful element to incorporate into your magic. Use that power to cast a protection spell that will endure for the year ahead.

YOU WILL NEED *gloves, a handful of fresh snow, a bowl, a white candle (a tealight candle will suffice) and matches.*

Wearing gloves, gather up a handful of fresh snow from outside and cup it in your hands to make a snowball. Place your snowball into the bowl, then light your white candle.

Visualize Chione's icy energy surrounding your home, creating a protective barrier. As the snow begins to melt, say aloud:

'Chione, goddess of snow,
guard my home and all within.
Melt away all harm,
let only safety enter in.'

Once the snow has melted, take the bowl outside and pour the water across the threshold of your home.

Winter love spell

On the coldest days, we need warmth most of all. This spell invites love into your life, welcoming in intimacy and connection.

YOU WILL NEED *2 large pinecones, 10 cloves, an orange or tangerine, a pinch each of ground ginger and ground cinnamon, red ribbon, scissors, a pink candle and matches.*

Take your pinecones and push five cloves between the scales or plates of each one. Peel the orange or tangerine, then cut the peel into pieces small enough to push between the pinecone scales.

Sprinkle each cone with ginger and cinnamon, then tie a piece of red ribbon around each pinecone, leaving enough ribbon at one end for hanging them.

Light the pink candle and place the pinecones in front of it. Say:

'I light this candle to bring love to my door. I ask the Winter Deities to bring me someone kind, caring, warm and honest, to love me as I am. The spell is cast; so mote it be.'

Leave the pinecones in place while the candle safely burns down. If there is any residual candle wax, wait until it's cool, then push little bits between the pinecone scales.

Hang the pinecones near to each other, either on your Christmas/Yule tree, or somewhere in your home where you will see them every day.

Winter herb bundle

Many winter spells call for herb smoke, and this herb bundle is imbued with the season's natural offerings.

YOU WILL NEED *dried herbs and greenery (such as mistletoe, pine needles and heather) and natural twine.*

Make sure your herbs are completely dry. Gather them into a bundle and tie tightly together with the twine. Bless the bundle by saying:

'One by one, you are powerful. Together you are mighty. Bless this herb stick to bring results. So be it.'

Keep your herb stick somewhere dry to use in future spells.

After burning your herb bundle, always collect the spent ash, as it will have absorbed the negative energy. Be sure to dispose of it away from your home.

Winter wellness brew

Ingredients like ginger, cinnamon, honey and lemon have been used for centuries to ward off illness and strengthen the body's natural defences. This brew calls on the power of Skaði (see page 15). Make it if you start to feel unwell during a full-moon phase.

YOU WILL NEED *your favourite hot chocolate powder, milk or water, a pinch each of ground ginger and ground cinnamon, 1 teaspoon honey and a squeeze of lemon juice.*

Make your hot chocolate with hot milk or water according to the packet instructions. Add the spices, honey and lemon and stir. As you do so, say the following words out loud:

'By the power of Skaði, I ask you to give me the strength to boost my health and wellbeing. So be it.'

Take your time drinking your healing hot drink.

Festive friendship charm

Winter gatherings bring strangers together. If you feel shy or anxious, this charm helps open your spirit to new connections, easing conversation and strengthening bonds. For best results, cast on a Sunday.

YOU WILL NEED *a blank postcard, a gold pen, a bay leaf, sticky tape and 30cm (12in) piece of gold ribbon.*

Write your wish for new friends on the postcard using the gold pen, including what qualities you'd love them to have. Stick the bay leaf on to the postcard using the tape, then roll it into a tube. Secure with the gold ribbon and leave on your bedroom windowsill for 24 hours.

Winter trade blessing

Winter's slower pace can make business feel uncertain, but magic can help open doors. This spell invites new opportunities, supporting career and business growth through the colder months. For best results, cast on a Thursday evening during a waxing-moon phase.

YOU WILL NEED *a piece of white card, a silver pen, 4 silver star stickers, your business card or a drawing of your logo, glue and a silver coin.*

On the card, use the silver pen to write down everything you want to manifest for your business or career. Do you need more clients? More money for stock? Extra staff? Better premises? Visualize exactly what it is you want and write it down.

Stick a silver star on each corner of the card, and glue your business card or logo into the middle. Stick the silver coin to the back of the card, then close your eyes and say the following words:

'This manifesto represents the wishes for my business. May my wishes be granted; may my dreams become reality. This is my wish; so be it.'

Keep your piece of card in a safe place wherever you work.

Pet protection spell

The dark season can bring unseen dangers to our animal companions. This spell shields them while they wander, keeping them safe until spring's return. For best results, cast at any time on a Tuesday or during a new-moon phase.

YOU WILL NEED *a rose-scented candle, a feather, a rose-scented incense stick, something belonging to your pet (such as a collar or some fur – you could also use a photograph) and matches.*

This spell should be performed in the garden if possible. Find a nice quiet space and arrange the objects in the following order – place the candle in the centre, place the feather behind the candle, the incense stick in front of the candle, and the object belonging to your pet in front of the incense stick. Light the candle first, followed by the incense stick.

Now say the following:

'Goddess, creator of nature, may you hear my call. Protect (name of pet) and all living creatures. No harm may come to all. So be it.'

Wave the object that belongs to your pet through the incense smoke, and do the same with the feather. Allow the candle to safely burn down. Keep the feather for future use. Your pet is now protected from predators or harm.

Repeat this spell once a month to keep your pet safe.

Winter broom

The broom, or besom, is one of the most iconic symbols of witchcraft. Traditionally, it represents both protection and purification, sweeping away negative energies and unwanted spirits from the home. In folklore, brooms were often used in rituals to mark sacred space, or even as symbols of transition. Many witches choose to craft or decorate brooms for each season, imbuing them with the unique energies of the time of year. A winter broom draws upon the resilience of nature to create a tool of protection and banishment for the darker months.

YOU WILL NEED *a long branch for the handle, foraged fallen twigs, secateurs, garden twine, white ribbon, a glue gun and glue, and decorations of your choosing (such as old pieces of jewellery).*

Make sure that all the wood you have collected is dry. Lay the long branch on the ground or a table, then gather all the twigs together and cut them so that they are equal lengths. They should be long enough to cover the last 15cm (6in) of the handle.

Begin by adding a few twigs to the branch, then tie some garden twine around them to secure them in place. Repeat this process until you have enough twigs to create the brush part of your broom.

When you're happy, you can start decorating. Begin by gluing the white ribbon to the top of the broom handle, then winding it all the way down to meet the brush part. Dab spots of glue along the handle to secure the ribbon.

Glue any decorations you like to the handle of your broom. When you are happy with the end result, place the broom on the floor, close your eyes and jump over it to activate the broom with your magical energy.

You now have your own winter broom to use for spells or in banishings. If you move home during this season, however, leave your broom behind and make a new one.

Winter's energy shield spell

The dark season can sometimes draw in people whose energy drains or unsettles us. This spell creates a protective shield against such influences, helping you guard your light through the winter months.

YOU WILL NEED *a dark blue or black candle and matches.*

Find a quiet time and place where you can sit for a while. Light your candle and look into the flame, imagining that the light is casting a protective shield around you. Sit for as long as you wish. Extinguish the candle when you feel ready.

Festive fortune spell

The festive season is made for celebration, yet not every outing flows smoothly. This spell blesses your evening with joy, luck and ease. Cast just before leaving for a gathering.

YOU WILL NEED *4 pink candles, a mirror, matches and your favourite lipstick.*

Place the candles in a line in front of your mirror and light them. Apply your favourite lipstick. Say:

'I have the confidence to have an amazing night tonight.'

Blow out the candles in one big breath to use again, then head out to enjoy a fabulous evening!

Winter travel protection charm

Travel in the harsher months has always carried a sense of risk. This protective spell calls upon Beira (see page 15), the great winter goddess of Scottish lore, who shapes the land and watches over journeys during the cold season. Cast the day before you're set to travel.

YOU WILL NEED *a sprig of heather, a small envelope and a pinch of salt.*

Heather is considered to be one of the luckiest seasonal plants, while the salt will provide protection for you and your fellow travellers.

Hold the sprig of heather between your palms, close your eyes and say:

'Beira, I call upon you to protect me on this trip I am about to take. May you always be by my side. May you always be my protector. So mote it be.'

Blow your energy into your palms, then put the heather and a pinch of salt into an envelope. Seal the envelope and keep it with your passport or travel documents.

Yuletide altar

An altar is a special place where you store all your witchy tools. It's helpful to adapt your altar to the changing seasons so that you have all the current resources and ingredients on hand for quick spellcasting. This Yuletide altar will help you focus on the blessings of the season. For best results, make your altar on or around Yule.

YOU WILL NEED *a nice table covering, lavender essential oil, sandalwood essential oil, peppermint essential oil, ylang ylang essential oil, a nice branch from a tree or a piece of driftwood (to represent earth), a candle (to represent fire), a small windchime (to represent wind), a bowl of salt water (to represent water), a sprig each of mistletoe and pine, a selection of crystals/wands/runes/cards, etc., and anything else you would like to add that's personal to you.*

Clean the area you are going to use as your altar, then lay down the table covering. Before putting anything on it, you need to purify the space with three drops of each of the essential oils. Allow the oils to seep into the tablecloth for a minute, then place your branch or driftwood on the table, followed by the candle, the chimes and the bowl of salt water.

Wave your hands over the altar and say:

'I bless this sacred space. So mote it be. This space created is just for me.'

You can now decorate it with the mistletoe and pine, along with your chosen crystals, cards, etc.

Family protection spell

When kin gather in your home during the festive season, they are both your source of joy and a responsibility. This rite protects not just you, but your entire household. For best results, cast just before Yule.

YOU WILL NEED *a red candle, a green candle, a silver candle, a gold candle, matches, your favourite music, white paper, scissors, a silver pen, a gold pen and glue.*

Place all your candles in a line in a safe place and light them in any order. Put on some fun music that everyone in your family likes. Fold a sheet of paper into quarters, then trim the unfolded edge into a curve to create a circle.

Keeping the paper folded, snip away at it to create a unique snowflake – you can find many how-to videos online. Make as many of these as you like, and the more creative you get with this project, the better.

Take the pens and write the names of anyone (human or animal) you want to protect on your snowflakes. The power is in you writing the names. Use the glue to stick the snowflakes to the windows in your home.

Allow the candles to burn down safely.

Magical Yule log

The Yule log is a centuries-old tradition focused on warmth, continuity and good fortune. By blessing and burning a log, you kindle prosperity for the year ahead. For best results, perform on or around Yule.

YOU WILL NEED *a dry log, roughly 15cm (6in) long, an old towel, a glue gun and glue, 3 yellow tealight candles (or white if you can't find yellow ones), some holly leaves (with berries, if possible), a sprig of mistletoe, gold and green biodegradable glitter, green ribbon, scissors, a piece of florist's foam and matches.*

Place the log on the towel to prevent it from rolling away. Using the glue gun, stick the tealights to the log, placing one at each end and one in the middle. Add the holly leaves and mistletoe and glue these on to the log.

Decorate the log with the glitter and the ribbon. Place the log on a table or somewhere safe and secure it with the florist's foam, cutting the foam to shape as needed. Use any remaining foliage to decorate the foam.

Light the three candles from left to right and say:

'On this Winter's Solstice, I call upon the light to bring forth prosperity, abundance, love and joy for the coming year. By the power of light, shine brightly on my path ahead. So mote it be.'

Allow the candles to safely burn down and place the Yule log outside your doorway for seven days to encourage good luck to come your way.

Yule runes

Runes are great for using alongside Tarot cards, oracles or any other divination tools. Runes carved or drawn at the Solstice carry special potency. This spell lets you inscribe seasonal symbols from the Elder Futhark, the oldest form of the runic alphabets, for protection, prosperity or guidance in the year to come. For best results, perform on or around Yule.

YOU WILL NEED *a white tealight candle, matches, 25 small, flat stones, a visual reference showing the 24 runes of the Elder Futhark, a permanent marker, clear nail varnish, a hessian bag.*

Light your candle in a calm space. On each stone, draw one rune symbol, leaving the final stone blank. Once the ink has dried, paint each stone with two layers of clear nail varnish, allowing them to dry between coats. Leave to dry completely, preferably on a sunny windowsill to absorb the sun's energy.

When the runes are dry, place them all together into your bag. You now have your very own set of Yule runes which can be used for divination and guidance, or for reflection and answers to a problem.

Happy home spell

When families gather for the festivities, tensions may rise with so many personalities under one roof. Craft this festive decoration to keep goodwill flowing in your home. For best results, cast any time before Yule.

YOU WILL NEED ***a wooden coat hanger, sprigs of mistletoe and fir, pinecones, a glue gun and glue and yellow ribbon.***

Spend some time decorating the coat hanger with your natural decorations, gluing them into place. Tie the yellow ribbon into a bow and add it to the hanger. Hang this in the doorway of the room in which you are gathering.

Yule Tarot reading

Tarot readings performed on Yule night have long been thought to reveal patterns for the year ahead, offering guidance, warnings and blessings. This 12-card spread mirrors the 12 months of the coming year, helping you step into the new cycle with clarity and purpose. For best results, perform on Yule night.

YOU WILL NEED ***a white tealight candle, matches, a deck of Tarot or oracle cards with a booklet of meanings (unless you already know them), salt, a journal and a pen.***

Light your candle and focus your mind on the deck of cards in your hands. Shuffle the cards until you feel ready to draw them. You need to pick a total of 12 cards. When you've chosen your cards, arrange them in four rows on a table. Before looking at any of them, cast a circle of salt around the cards to lock in protection. You can now turn over the first card, and read them from left to right, row by row.

The cards represent the following:

1 – here and now
2 – what has passed
3 – your hopes and dreams
4 – three months ahead
5 – what you need to work on
6 – what is causing unease
7 – action you need to take
8 – six months ahead
9 – actions and guidance
10 – nine months ahead
11 – moving forwards
12 – overall reading

Be sure to journal about your reading and any insights that emerge. Above all, remember to let your intuition guide you as you read the cards.

Yule cake spell

Blessing a Yule cake turns sweetness into a charm for joy and abundance that can be shared with family or guests. Perform on or around Yule.

YOU WILL NEED *an un-iced fruit cake (or sponge cake, if you prefer), edible rice paper, an icing pen, a spatula or spoon, icing and edible decorations.*

Bake or buy your cake of choice and place it on the kitchen side in preparation. Take the icing pen and edible rice paper and write the following words on the paper:

'Blessed are all who eat this cake, which with love and care I bake.'

Place the edible paper on top of the cake, then cover it in icing and decorate as you wish. As you decorate your cake, say the following words:

'May this bring joy and magic to those who eat, merry be and merry meet.'

Offer a slice of cake to anyone you wish to bless.

Sanctuary spell

Sometimes solitude is the best gift you can give yourself. This spell grants you space to recharge during the festivities. For best results, cast on a Saturday, preferably during a waning-moon phase.

YOU WILL NEED *a dark blue candle, 5 drops of lavender essential oil, 1 teaspoon salt, a heatproof dish and matches.*

Anoint the candle by rubbing the lavender oil into it. Scatter the salt over the base of the heatproof dish, then stand the candle in the salt. Light the candle, imagining peace and quiet as you do so. Allow the candle to safely burn down, then dispose of the salt.

Yule wish poppet

Poppet dolls have been used in magical practices for hundreds of years as powerful manifestation tools. This spell invites you to craft a poppet to hold a heartfelt wish, empowering it with Winter Solstice energy. For best results, perform on or around Yule.

YOU WILL NEED *a pen, felt in your favourite colour, scissors, a sewing needle and thread, cotton wool and a small piece of paper.*

Draw the outline of a human figure on to the felt with your pen and cut it out twice. Sew the two outlines together around the edges, leaving a small gap at the top of the head, then stuff with cotton wool. Draw on eyes, nose and a smile.

Write your wish on a small piece of paper, roll it up and pop it into the gap on your poppet doll's head. Sew up the doll, then place her somewhere where you will see her everyday.

North Star guidance meditation

The North Star, Polaris, has long been a beacon of guidance for sailors, travellers and witches. It is easily visible on clear nights in the Northern Hemisphere, and is one of the brightest stars in the sky. This spell calls upon the North Star to bring clarity when you feel lost, helping you align your inner compass with the cosmos. For best results, perform under a clear sky, away from the glow of city lights and town pollution.

YOU WILL NEED *a clear night, a blanket, a pillow or cushion and a warm drink.*

Once you have located the North Star in the sky, lay out your blanket and pillow, then lie down and get comfortable. Look up at the bright star, then close your eyes and silently ask the cosmos for guidance with a particular problem or situation. Remain where you are for as long as you like. Have a warm drink to hand and allow yourself to just be for the moment.

You will find you have more clarity when you return home.

Holiday cracker change spell

The playful ritual of the holiday cracker becomes magical in your hands. Use this spell to spark transformation, welcoming fresh energy and new beginnings. For best results, perform in the evening on or around Yule.

YOU WILL NEED *an open fire/firepit, matches, a bay leaf, a holly leaf, scissors, a small bowl, a red pen and a small piece of paper.*

Light your fire. Take the holly leaf and bay leaf and cut them up into tiny pieces, then place them in the bowl. Think of one word that represents the change you are seeking. This could be something like 'confidence', 'patience', 'strength' or 'wealth'. Write the word in red pen on the piece of paper.

Take the small clippings of holly and bay leaves and place them into the middle of the paper. Roll the paper into a scroll and twist the two ends, so that it looks like a tiny cracker. Hold the 'cracker' between your hands, close your eyes and imagine the word you've written in red in your mind.

Throw the paper cracker into the firepit and watch it crackle and burn. The smoke from the cracker will rise into the universe and your wish will be granted for the coming year.

♥ Yule candle blessing

At Yule, the darkest night of the year gives way to the returning light. It is a time of togetherness, warmth and gratitude for the people who bring love and joy into our lives. One beautiful way to honour this season is by exchanging candles, sharing both physical light and the symbolic spark of affection and unity. Perform this group spell on or around Yule.

YOU WILL NEED *friends/family, several white tealight candles (one for each person) and matches.*

Stand in a circle (or opposite each other if there are only two of you) and begin the spell with one person saying the following words out loud:

'Upon this night,
we give this light,
to bring together our love so bright.
Upon this night,
we become one.
Love we now exchange. So mote it be.'

The person who spoke can now light their own candle, before lighting the candle of the person on their right. Repeat this until all the candles are lit.

Remain in the circle for a few minutes, grateful for the love that you all share. The person who began the spell can now close the circle by blowing out the candle of the person on their right. Continue around the circle until all the candles are blown out.

Enjoy the evening with your friends or family.

★ Winter Solstice gratitude ritual

The Winter Solstice is a threshold moment. This ritual helps you pause to honour all you have received so that your spirit is open to future blessings. For best results, perform on or around the Winter Solstice.

YOU WILL NEED *a white candle, matches, paper and a pen.*

Find a quiet time. Light the candle and take out your paper and pen. Write down everything you are grateful for: all your blessings from the past 12 months. Read your list out loud and feel thankful for all you have.

Place the sheet of paper under your pillow for 28 days to magically bring new blessings to be thankful for.

Yuletide purging spell

Yule is not only about celebration but also release. This rite helps you banish what no longer serves you, clearing space for new blessings as the light returns. For best results, perform on Yule.

YOU WILL NEED *a green pen, paper, a few sprigs of mistletoe, green ribbon, an open fire/fire pit and matches.*

Take some time to think about what it is you wish to purge from your life, and what you would like to manifest into your life for the next 12 months. With the green pen, write down what you wish to get rid of on one side of the paper, followed by what you would like to attract into your life instead. Place the mistletoe in the centre of the paper and roll it up into a scroll. Secure the scroll with the green ribbon.

Light your fire and, when you feel ready, throw the scroll into the flames. As you watch it burn, say the words:

'Old Man Winter, I give you my request on this 21st day, to grant my wishes, and do as I say. So be it this Yuletide, so mote it be.'

Solstice prosperity wreath

As the Winter Solstice passes and days begin to lengthen, life moves once again towards growth. This spell calls in prosperity, aligning your path with the abundance of returning light. Perform on or around the Winter Solstice, during a waxing-moon phase.

YOU WILL NEED *a plain Christmas/Yule wreath (or you can make one - see page 19), several pine sprigs, 5 cinnamon sticks, dried orange slices, small pinecones, glue gun and glue, natural twine, red and green ribbon, peppermint essential oil and any additional decorations you wish.*

Take your wreath and wind the pine sprigs securely into it. Next add the cinnamon sticks, pinecones and orange slices, gluing them into place. Wind the twine and ribbon around the wreath, then sprinkle the whole thing with the peppermint oil as you say the following:

'On this special day of Yule, I am blessed with prosperity for the coming months. I may now hibernate without worry as prosperity flows my way. So mote it be.'

You can add a personal touch to your wreath with necklaces, crystals or other items personal to you if you wish.

Hang your wreath either inside or outside your home.

★ Winter reflection spell

Before charging forward, it is wise to pause. This spell supports reflection on the year that has just passed, helping you honour your achievements over the last 12 months. Perform on or around New Year's Eve.

YOU WILL NEED ***a white or silver candle, a mason jar, water, a small pinecone, several evergreen sprigs, a freezer and matches.***

Gently warm the bottom of the candle so that the wax melts a little, then secure it inside the mason jar. Pour a couple of inches of water into the jar, being careful not to dislodge the candle. Add the pinecone and evergreen sprigs to the jar too.

Carefully place your jar in the freezer and allow the water to freeze.

Once it has frozen, take the jar to a quiet place. Allow the ice to thaw a little to prevent the glass from breaking, then light the candle. As it burns down, think about all you have achieved in the past 12 months, and give thanks to the universe for keeping you safe and protected. The candle will extinguish itself as it meets the melting ice.

Bad-habit breaker spell

We all fall into unhelpful patterns now and then. This spell helps release those habits that no longer serve you, clearing space for healthier choices to take root. For best results, perform during a waning-moon phase – a day with a strong breeze is best.

YOU WILL NEED ***1 teaspoon ground black pepper, 1 teaspoon ground cinnamon, 1 teaspoon sugar, 1 teaspoon mixed dried herbs, a bowl, a bare hawthorn twig and 3 white feathers.***

Add the pepper, cinnamon, sugar and herbs to the bowl one at a time, and use your hawthorn twig to mix them all together. As you mix them, say:

'Bad habit, banish, banish, banish.'

Take the white feathers and arrange them in a triangle shape around the outside of the bowl. Stir the mixture again, repeating:

'Bad habit, banish, banish, banish.'

Wait ten minutes, then take your dish and feathers outside.

Find out which way the wind is blowing, and throw the contents of the bowl into the air so that the wind carries them away. Say the following words:

'Elements of the wind, carry these bad habits far away, so that they may never find their way home again.'

Finally, throw the feathers into the wind, then turn clockwise three times before walking away.

Release guilt spell

Guilt can weigh heavily, keeping us tied to the past. This spell helps release that burden so you can learn from your mistakes and move forward with clarity and peace. For best results, perform during a waning-moon phase.

YOU WILL NEED *a black candle, matches, a small spray bottle, water, 3 sprigs of dried lavender, a white candle and 1 teaspoon bicarbonate of soda.*

Find a time when you can have half an hour to yourself. Light the black candle and, as it burns down, reflect on what you feel guilty about and how it may have affected others in your life. Allow the emotions to come and go. Allow the candle to safely burn down, then dispose of any remaining wax in the bin.

Fill your spray bottle with water, then add the sprigs of dried lavender and shake well. Light the white candle and, as you do so, ask yourself for forgiveness and ask for the forgiveness of others. Visualize a white light hovering over your head and travelling down through your body, cleansing you of guilt and creating a fresh start.

When the candle has safely burned down, spray yourself all over with the lavender water. Next, take off the shoes you are wearing and scatter ½ teaspoon of bicarbonate of soda into each shoe. This will make sure that all your guilt is absolved.

Ancestral guidance spell

Winter's quiet is a powerful space for reflection and remembrance. This ice-jar spell invites guidance from your ancestors, helping you draw strength and wisdom from your lineage. For best results, cast on a Sunday evening, having prepared for the spell earlier in the day.

YOU WILL NEED *a glass jar or bottle, fresh snow or tap water, 2 sprigs of rosemary (or a pinch of dried rosemary), 2 mint leaves (or a pinch of dried mint), a squeeze of lemon juice, a freezer, a white candle and matches.*

Fill the jar with either fresh water or fresh, clean snow from outside. Add the rosemary, mint and lemon juice, and shake well. Place the jar in the freezer for an hour, or until the water is frozen.

Remove the jar and allow it to thaw at room temperature. Light your candle and stare into the flame. Take a sip of your magic water and say:

'I call upon my ancestors to connect with me now. I ask that you give me guidance and advice with (name the topic). I wait for you to come to me.'

Continue to sip the water and gaze into the flame of the candle. Signs that your ancestors are trying to connect are when the flame flares up or starts to flicker. Close your eyes and listen to your inner voice. You will be given the answers or guidance you need to hear. Extinguish the candle when you feel ready and pour away any remaining water.

★ New year manifestation spell

The start of the new year is the perfect moment to set intentions. This spell channels the momentum of new beginnings to draw your desires closer. Perform on New Year's Eve at midnight, or at any time on New Year's Day.

YOU WILL NEED *white paper, a red pen, a hole punch, a red poinsettia plant in a pot and water.*

Sit for a while and contemplate what you want in your life for the new year. Write it down as if you are already experiencing this exciting new change. For example, if you want to be a better cook, write down, 'I love cooking. It feels so good to make amazing food whenever I want.'

Hole-punch the paper to turn your words into confetti, then scatter these little paper circles on to the compost of the poinsettia. Sprinkle the soil with a little water – these plants don't like to be overwatered, so be sparing here, adding just enough water to activate the spell. If cared for properly, poinsettia plants will survive through to spring, allowing time for this spell to work.

Continue to care for the plant. As the paper decomposes, your wish will be sent to the universe.

♥ New year blessings spell

This blessing spell welcomes good fortune for your loved ones in the 12 months ahead. Perform outside or in a well-ventilated space on or around New Year's Day.

YOU WILL NEED *a selection of greeting cards or gift tags from gifts you received during the festive season, scissors, a cauldron or fireproof pot, the peel of an orange or satsuma, a white tealight candle, matches and a wand or stick.*

Cut the cards and gift tags into small pieces. As you do so, remember who took the trouble to write to you and think of them fondly.

Tip the pieces into your cauldron or fireproof pot, then add the citrus peel. Light your candle, then mix the pieces of paper and the orange peel with your wand or stick as you say:

'Blessings to you, and you, and you too.'

Once all the pieces are mixed together, carefully light a few pieces of paper using a match. The flames will soon spread to the other pieces of paper and the citrus peel. Wait until everything in the pot has burned and cooled, then scatter the ashes in your garden. Your loved ones will be protected for the coming year.

New Year's Eve binding spell

This spell binds any difficulties from the past, helping you overcome your bad habits and start the new year afresh. Perform on New Year's Eve.

YOU WILL NEED *a length of red cord (long enough to tie around your wrist twice).*

Sit quietly and think about habits or behaviours you would like to leave behind you. For each one, tie a knot into the length of red cord. As you do so, say:

'I bind (name the habit or behaviour).'

When you're ready, tie the cord around the wrist of your dominant hand.

Clarity dream spell

At this introspective time of year, some bigger life questions may arise. This spell grants you divine clarity as you sleep. For best results, perform in the evening before bed.

YOU WILL NEED *paper and a yellow pen.*

Think of your question and write it on the paper using the yellow pen. Now say:

'As I travel into sleep,
I'll find the answer in the deep.'

Place the paper under your pillow – the answer will come to you by morning.

Positive mantras charm

Thoughts are power, and when we dwell on negative things, we only make that outcome more likely. This repetition spell will help you train your brain to only repeat positive mantras.

YOU WILL NEED *a tealight candle, matches, paper and a pen.*

Light your candle and think about what you desire right now – for example, a successful job interview or a positive first date. Starting at the top left-hand side of the paper, begin writing one sentence that sums up your request, using language that suggests it is already happening. So, if it's a positive job interview, you might write:

'My interview is a great success.'

Continue to write your chosen sentence over and over again, as if you were writing lines at school. Keep going until you have filled up one side of the paper, then repeat again for the other side. When you get to the bottom of the paper, the very last line should read:

'So mote it be.'

Blow out your candle and keep the sheet of paper with you until your wish comes true.

★ Dream-job manifestation spell

If your career feels stagnant, this spell calls upon the Morrigan, Irish goddess of war, fate and sovereignty, to help you strategize so you can attract a role aligned with your true calling. For best results, cast on a Thursday during a full-moon phase.

YOU WILL NEED *a piece of green paper, a gold pen, 3 holly leaves, scissors, 1 teaspoon dried sage, 1 gold or silver candle and matches.*

Draw a large pentagram (a five-pointed star within a circle, see page 124) in the centre of your piece of paper using the gold pen. Inside the pentagram, write down everything you want in a new job. Is it part-time or full-time? What does it pay? What are your hours? Is it in an office or outdoors?

Cut the holly leaves into tiny pieces and place these and the dried sage into the centre of the pentagram.

Light the candle as you say the following words out loud:

'Goddess Morrigan, hear my plea today. Send me a job according to my needs, a job I will love. So below, so above, so mote it be.'

Allow the candle to safely burn down, then carefully take the paper to an open window and blow the holly and herbs out of the window.

Pentagram snow angel

The pentagram (a five-pointed star within a circle, see page 124) symbolizes the connection between nature's five elements: earth, water, fire, air and spirit. Snow, meanwhile, is a magical substance, with every flake unique. This spell combines the two, and also allows you to connect to your inner child as you form a pentagram snow angel. In doing so, you call upon winter's sacred geometry for protection and renewal. Perform this spell outdoors in fresh snow.

YOU WILL NEED *warm clothes, snow and a stick.*

Wrap up warm and find an undisturbed area of snow. Using a stick, draw a large pentagram into the snow, making sure it's big enough for you to lie on top of it. Lie down on your back on top of the pentagram. Wave your arms and legs as you would when making a snow angel. As you do so, say the following words:

'I call upon Beira, the queen of winter, to bring forth only good luck from here on. Protect me and make me heal; take my wishes and make them real.'

Stand up and repeat the process twice more, so that you end up with three pentagram snow angels in a row. Once the snow melts, your luck will start to increase.

If you don't have snow in your country, or have very little of it, you can cast this spell in sand instead. Once the sea or natural elements wash away the pentagram sand angels, you will see your luck improving.

Twelfth Night luck spell

According to folklore, ivy is a plant of recovery and protection from evil; if it grows outside your home, you will be protected for as long as you live there. This spell draws upon that magic to refresh your fortunes and invite in luck for the year ahead. Perform on or around Twelfth Night (5 or 6 January).

YOU WILL NEED *3 ivy leaves, a glass bowl and a bottle of spring water.*

Pluck three leaves from an ivy plant and give thanks to the plant. Fill the glass bowl with the bottle of spring water and hover your hand over the water for a minute to send your energy into it. Hold the first leaf in your dominant hand for a moment while visualizing your bad luck ending and good luck coming back into your life, then place the leaf into the water. Repeat with the other two leaves.

Leave the bowl of water and leaves outside for 24 hours. Strain the water the following day and let the leaves dry, then put them into your pocket or purse.

Pathfinder's spell

When faced with choices, hesitation drains your power. This spell clears indecision, endowing you with the wisdom to act boldly.

YOU WILL NEED *2 plant pots, a pen, compost, 2 hyacinth bulbs and water.*

Consider the choice you are trying to make, and write one option on each plant pot. Fill them with compost and plant one bulb in each pot. Sprinkle with water, saying:

'Decisions, decisions, time to show,
let me know as you grow.'

Place the pots in a dark place. Whichever bulb blooms first will reveal your answer.

Simple cinnamon money spell

This straightforward spell uses just one simple storecupboard staple to help restore your festive funds.

YOU WILL NEED *1 teaspoon dried cinnamon.*

Tip the dried cinnamon into the palm of your hand. Stand outside your open front door and blow the spice into your home.

You will have extra money coming in before the end of the month. Repeat on the first day of every month if you wish.

★ Snow manifestation spell

This manifestation spell channels the power of snowfall, allowing your wishes to crystallize and take form. Perform on a snowy day.

YOU WILL NEED *a small piece of rice paper, a pencil and fresh snow (or a handful of built-up ice from your freezer).*

Sit for a while and think about what it is you want to manifest into your life right now. Write it down on the rice paper with your pencil, and really visualize it happening. No dream is too big, so go for it – the only proviso is that you really believe it's achievable. Take your time and consider any consequences your wish might have on others.

Go out into the snow (or carefully scoop a handful of ice from your freezer), then mould a snowball. Before you complete the snowball, push the rice paper inside, then add more snow so that it is completely hidden.

When you are happy with your snowball, take it outside and throw it high into the air, asking the universe to grant your wish. Leave it where it lands.

As the snowball melts and the rice paper dissolves, you will see new opportunities arising that will show that your wish is on its way.

Luck refresher spell

In winter's stillness, our fortunes can feel stagnant too. This simple spell can turn the tide, sweeping away misfortune and opening your path to brighter days. It calls upon Lord and Lady Wintertime, considered in English folklore to be the governors of winter.

YOU WILL NEED *a green candle, a silver pin, a green pen and matches.*

Place your candle somewhere it will not get disturbed for the next nine days. Use the silver pin to score horizontal lines into the candle, dividing it into nine equal parts. Now close your eyes and stick the pin into the candle. Next, take your green pen and write the word 'luck' in each segment on the candle.

On the first night of the full moon, light the candle and repeat the following six times:

'Lord and Lady of the Wintertime,
hear my plea.
Make my fortune change for me.
Banish now my past misfortune, and
return good luck, during this full moon.'

Allow the first segment of the candle to safely burn down, then blow out the flame. Bow to the candle and silently give thanks to the Lord and Lady.

Repeat this process for the next eight nights at around the same time each night. When the pin falls out, it is a sign that any bad luck has ended.

If there is any wax left after the nine days, bury it in your garden or a flowerpot. Your luck will now be renewed. Keep the silver pin in case you wish to cast the spell again.

Subtle banishment spell

Sometimes, protection requires discretion. This spell banishes a negative influence without drawing attention to itself. For best results, perform on a Saturday during a waning-moon phase.

YOU WILL NEED *a black candle, matches, a small piece of paper, a black pen, a small padlock and key, a bowl or saucer, an ice cube and a black cloth.*

Light your candle, then write the name of the person on the paper using the black pen. Open the padlock and place the piece of paper where the lock bar will clamp down when it's locked again. Push the lock together to trap the piece of paper in the padlock.

Next, place the padlock into a bowl or saucer and place the ice cube on top of the padlock. Cover the bowl with the black cloth and say:

'(Name), you are now blocked and locked out of my life for good. No longer may your energy affect mine. You have been banished, goodbye.'

Wait for the candle to safely burn down and for the ice cube to melt on the padlock. When this is done, throw the padlock into a bin away from your house and pour the water down the toilet.

Winter charm bag

This spell creates a bag of seasonal blessings, with lavender for good health, mint for prosperity and allspice to indicate an exciting time ahead. The charm also harnesses the power of Euphrosyne, the Greek goddess of joy, mirth and good cheer. For best results, perform on a Sunday evening.

YOU WILL NEED *a yellow candle, matches, a handful of dried lavender, a handful of dried mint, a handful of ground allspice, a yellow charm bag, 2 white winter rose petals, lavender essential oil and yellow ribbon.*

Light your candle, then combine the lavender, mint and allspice in the charm bag. Anoint each of the rose petals with a drop of lavender oil, then add these to the bag too. Tie the charm bag closed with the yellow ribbon and say the following words:

'Goddess Euphrosyne, I call upon you to bring forth the joy and laughter that is missing from my life. May you and your sisters bless me now with this happy charm, to bring close the fun and happiness that has been lacking. I thank you; so mote it be.'

Allow the candle to safely burn down and carry your happy charm bag with you for at least the next 28 days. You will soon begin to feel much happier.

Friendship pause spell

Friendships, like all relationships, need space to breathe. This spell grants a pause when you feel uncertain, allowing you time to reflect on whether a friend is supporting your growth or holding you back. For best results, cast on a Friday, during a new-moon phase.

YOU WILL NEED *a stick about 30cm (12in) long, a black pen and a stream.*

Think about the person or people you feel you need to take a break from, and whether they are bringing anything positive to your life. Do you feel like you might be more yourself if they weren't in the picture right now? When you're happy with your decision, write your own name on one end of the stick and the other person's name (or names) at the other end.

Go for a walk with your stick and find a stream or some form of running water. Hold the stick in your hands and say:

'I'm taking a break from you right now. I mean you no harm, but I need time without you. I send love and blessings your way, so that you too can grow without me for a while. So mote it be – one, two, three.'

On the count of three, snap the stick in half and throw both halves into the running water. Turn your back on them and walk away without looking back.

You will now be free to have a break from this person or people and reflect on what you truly need.

Banish gossip spell

When different groups gather, sometimes gossip circles can form. This spell silences unkind talk. For best results, perform during a waning-moon phase.

YOU WILL NEED *a slip of paper, a black pen, a plastic container (such as an ice-cream tub), a knife, a red pepper, a green pepper, an onion, 1 teaspoon ground black pepper, a spiky holly leaf, a jug, water and a freezer.*

Write the name of the person who has been gossiping about you on the slip of paper in black ink and place it in the container. Chop up the peppers and onion, and scatter them over the piece of paper. Add the black pepper and holly leaf. Fill a jug with water and slowly pour it into the container. As you do so, say the following words:

'May your tongue be sour from all your gossiping; may your words be returned to you. May you take back the pain and harm no one again. It is so.'

Place the container and its contents in the freezer for 24 hours. Afterwards, take the container out of the freezer and go outside. Drop the container on the ground so that the frozen mixture smashes into pieces. Finally, sweep the mixture away from your home.

★ Full-moon gratitude ritual

A full moon truly shines against a cold, crisp winter sky. This ritual draws on her light, filling you with gratitude to welcome future blessings. For best results, perform on the second night of a full-moon phase.

YOU WILL NEED *your favourite drink (fruit tea is a good choice for this spell), a white candle, a handful of dried lavender, a handful of dried jasmine flowers (available from health stores), salt and matches.*

Make your favourite drink, then take it to your altar or a quiet space to perform the spell. Place the candle in front of you, then sprinkle a circle of lavender around the candle, followed by a circle of jasmine flowers and finally a circle of salt, so you are left with a three-layered circle.

Light the candle and, as you sip your drink, consider how lucky we are to be living on this planet called Earth. Say the following words:

'I thank the gods and goddesses of the full moon for providing me with (three things that you are grateful for). I thank the lady of the moon for the power you have given me on this most potent night. I give blessings and thanks to you all; so be it.'

Sit in gratitude until the candle safely burns down.

Freeze them out spell

When someone's presence in your life becomes toxic, you can halt their impact on you without direct confrontation. This spell freezes their effect on your life. For best results, perform during a waning-moon phase.

YOU WILL NEED *paper, a black pen, a long icicle (or block one end of a straw, fill it with water and pop it in the freezer to make your own) and a freezer.*

Write the name of the person that you want to freeze out on your sheet of paper. Over the top of their name, draw a large pentagram (a five-pointed star within a circle, see page 124). Visualize the person as you wrap the paper around the icicle or frozen straw, and say the following words:

'This wintertime, I freeze you out.
I do this now, with no doubt.
No longer will you take up room in my mind;
no longer will you be unkind.
Be gone, be gone, from this day forth,
by the power of the south, west, east and north.
So be it this day.'

Place the wrapped icicle into your freezer and leave it there for 48 hours. Once this time has passed, take the icicle out of the freezer and dispose of it as far away from your home as possible. You can throw it into a river or a lake, or bury it in a forest or a field. As the icicle thaws and the paper degrades back into the earth, the person you were thinking about will disappear from your life.

Protection pin

This spell transforms an everyday object into a ward against harm; one you can carry discreetly into the year ahead.

YOU WILL NEED *a large safety pin (the bigger, the better), 6 small blue beads and 1 clove.*

Hold the safety pin in your hand until it feels warm. Thread three of the beads on to the pin, followed by the clove, then three more beads. Pin this to the inside of your top, trousers or skirt. You will be protected every time you wear this protection pin.

Banish bad dreams spell

The long, dark nights of winter can sometimes invite uneasy dreams. This spell calls on Apollo, god of light and healing, to drive away troubling visions and restore peace to your sleep. For best results, cast during a waning-moon phase.

YOU WILL NEED *2 sprigs of mistletoe, a white tealight candle and matches.*

Place one sprig of mistletoe outside your bedroom door and the other sprig anywhere inside your bedroom. Light your tealight candle and silently ask Apollo to protect you from any further bad dreams.

Allow the candle to safely burn down. Leave the mistletoe in place until you have pleasant dreams again.

Power rebalance spell

The winter season is a time for reflecting and learning lessons. Perhaps you gave away too much of your power to others – this spell will help you take it back. For best results, cast this spell on any evening during a full-moon phase.

YOU WILL NEED *a pen, 3 bay leaves, 3 white tealight candles, matches, a pinch of ground cinnamon, a pinch of ground ginger, salt and a small bowl.*

Write the word 'I've' on the first bay leaf, the word 'got' on the second bay leaf and the word 'this' on the third bay leaf. Place each bay leaf under a tealight candle and light the candles in the order of the words in the sentence: 'I've got this.' As you do so, say the following:

'By the power within me, by the power within me,
I bring forth my true control.
No longer will I allow anyone to take it away from me.
I've got this – so mote it be.'

While you allow the candles to safely burn down, combine the cinnamon, ginger and salt in the bowl and mix them using the index finger of your dominant hand.

When the candles have burned down, place the first leaf by your front door, the second by your back door and the third under your bed. Sprinkle the mixture from your bowl across the threshold to your home.

★ Winter inner-wisdom spell

Midwinter invites us to look inward. This spell sharpens intuition, helping you hear the quiet wisdom that emerges in stillness. For best results, perform before you go to sleep.

YOU WILL NEED *a lavender-scented candle, a sachet of dried lavender or mugwort, a notebook and a pen.*

Light your candle an hour before going to bed, and ask out loud for signs and messages to come to you while you sleep. Place the herb sachet under your pillow and blow out the candle before you go to bed. Keep the notebook and pen beside you so you can record any dreams or messages you receive in the night.

Banish the winter blues spell

This spell helps lift feelings of melancholy and restores emotional balance during the darker months. For best results, cast on a Saturday night.

YOU WILL NEED *gloves, a handful of fresh stinging nettles (before they have flowered), a mug, a bare hawthorn twig, hot water, ½ teaspoon ground cinnamon, ½ teaspoon ground ginger, a tea strainer, a spray bottle (optional).*

Note: Do not drink nettle tea if you take blood thinners.

Wearing gloves, gather a handful of fresh nettles (these can be found in most hedgerows) and place in the mug. Wash your hawthorn twig under the tap.

Pour hot water over the nettles in the mug, then add the cinnamon and ginger.

Allow the nettle tea to steep for 5 minutes, then stir in a clockwise direction with the hawthorn stick as you say:

'Winter blues are gone today,
replaced by joy every day.
Gone are my worries, gone are my troubles,
replaced by joyous days that are doubled.'

Strain the nettles from your tea and allow it to cool. Traditionally, witches would now drink the tea, but if you prefer, you can cool it completely, transfer it to a spray bottle and spritz yourself with it instead. The tea will keep for a couple of days if refrigerated, at which point you can dispose of it down the sink. Repeat whenever you're feeling blue.

Stay-away spell

Not everyone deserves access to your energy. This spell establishes a barrier, ensuring unwanted presences keep their distance. For best results, perform during a waning-moon phase.

YOU WILL NEED *gloves, secateurs, brambles, a dish and a pinch of salt and ground black pepper.*

Wearing gloves, use your secateurs to carefully cut some thorny brambles. Place the brambles in the dish, then add the salt and pepper. As you do so, think about the person you wish to stay out of your life. Place the bowl outside your home. The person won't bother you again.

Bonfire transformation spell

Even on the coldest days, flames carry great power. This spell harnesses fire's transformative power to ignite your desires. For best results, perform during a full-moon phase.

YOU WILL NEED *an open fire or a candle and matches.*

Light your fire or candle and sit in front of it on a cushion with your legs crossed. Keep your spine straight but relaxed.

Close your eyes and take a deep breaths in for the count of three, then slowly exhale for the count of four. Repeat this three times. Say to yourself:

'I am fine, everything is fine, all is well.'

Open your eyes and stare into the flame of either the fire or the candle, and visualize the power of the fire radiating into your body, eliminating all negative thoughts and feelings. Repeat three times:

'I am fine, everything is fine, all is well.'

Now visualize everything you wish for coming to you through the orange flame. Keep deep-breathing and repeating your magical mantra for as long as you like. When you feel happy and relaxed, allow the fire or candle to safely burn down on its own. You have now told your subconscious that you are powerful and can achieve, do and be anything you wish.

Winter slumber spell

The long, dark nights of the colder months are perfect for deep rest and healing sleep. Yet sometimes our minds won't switch off, leaving us restless. This simple bedtime spell uses lavender and candle magic to quiet your thoughts, soothe your spirit and invite peaceful dreams. For best results, perform it about an hour before bed.

YOU WILL NEED *a purple candle, lavender essential oil, a cotton ball or pad and matches.*

Anoint the candle with a few drops of lavender oil, then add a few more drops to the cotton ball or pad. Turn off any artificial lighting and light the candle. Looking at the flame, sing the following words as if you were singing a lullaby:

'Tonight I sing a lullaby
and send my worries to the sky.
Tonight my request is deep;
tonight I'll rest while I sleep.'

Spend as long as you like meditating on the flame of the candle until you begin to feel relaxed and tired. Blow out the candle and place the lavender-infused cotton ball on your pillow.

Banish bad luck spell

When misfortune clings too tightly in the dark winter months, this spell severs its grip, clearing the way for brighter turns of fate. For best results, perform during a new-moon phase.

YOU WILL NEED *1 teaspoon dried rosemary, 1 teaspoon salt, juice of 1 lemon or lime and a paper towel.*

Think about all the bad luck that has come your way lately as you tip the dried rosemary into the palm of your dominant hand. Next, add the salt to your palm, then squeeze the juice from the lemon or lime over the top.

Now rub your hands together over a sink, as if you were washing them.

Repeat the following words out loud three times:

'Be gone, be gone, bad luck of mine.
Go back to where I cannot find.
You are no longer invited, I banish your strife.
Be gone, be gone, out of my life.'

Rub the mixture all over your hands, then wiggle your fingers in the air to show you mean magical business.

Rinse the mixture from your hands and let it run down the sink, then dry your hands with the paper towel. Bad luck will be returned to its source, and only good luck will come to you now.

Frozen burdens release spell

Emotions are powerful, but sometimes they weigh us down. This spell uses the strength of ice to help you release negative emotions and regain emotional balance. For best results, perform during a waning-moon phase.

YOU WILL NEED *a paper cup, warm water, a small piece of paper, a pen, a freezer, a bowl and salt.*

Fill the paper cup with warm water (this freezes quicker than cold water).

On the paper, write down what you wish to release or a negative emotion that is not serving you, such as guilt, shame, jealousy or anger. Place the paper into the cup and put it in the freezer. Set your intention to freeze any negative emotion from yourself.

After a few hours, return to the freezer and take out the cup. Peel away the paper cup so you are left with a frozen block containing your scrap of paper. Put this into a bowl, then take it outside and sprinkle with salt. Allow the frozen block to melt away. Once it has melted, take out the slip of paper and throw it in the bin. Pour the water on to the ground. You have now released the negative emotion.

Snow's strength spell

Snow carries the quiet strength of winter; it falls gently yet transforms the land, cleansing and renewing everything it touches. Call on Chione (see page 15) to help clear away illness and return vitality during the colder months.

YOU WILL NEED ***a cup of fresh, clean snow (or ice cubes from the freezer), a saucepan and a wand or stick.***

Place your cup of snow into the saucepan and melt it over a very low heat. As it melts, wave your wand or stick over the pan and say:

'I call upon Chione, goddess of snow.
Release, release, release.
Heal, heal, heal.
With your strength, my wellness grows.'

Repeat these words until all the snow has melted. Once cooled, drink the snow water or use it to make your morning tea or coffee.

Peace tree spell

Even when its branches are bare, a tree still holds life force deep within. This spell draws on that ancient strength and wisdom to calm inner turmoil and restore peace.

YOU WILL NEED *a large tree (such as oak or horse chestnut), a white tealight candle, matches and white ribbon (enough to wrap around the trunk of the tree).*

Place the tealight candle at the base of the tree and light it. Walk around it in a clockwise direction nine times and say:

'Peace is restored to me; I now feel free.
By the power of nature, by the power of this tree,
bliss is now returned to me.'

Tie the white ribbon in a bow around the full base of the tree trunk. Leave the ribbon in place until the candle burns safely down, then remove the candle and ribbon. The tree will grant your wish for peace.

Healing gift basket

This spell infuses a gift basket with energies of comfort and renewal, perfect for anyone feeling under the weather. For best results, perform on a Friday during a full-moon phase.

YOU WILL NEED *a wicker basket, a rose quartz crystal, an amethyst crystal, a clear quartz crystal, seasonal fruit and vegetables, some sweet treats, a potted miniature winter rose (or other seasonal plant) and yellow ribbon.*

Place all the items on a windowsill that catches the moonlight, and leave them there for one night under the full moon.

The next day, hold each crystal in the palm of your hand for a few minutes and visualize healing power radiating from you to the crystal. Place the crystals into the basket. Arrange the fruit and vegetables in the basket too, along with the sweet treats, then finally add the winter rose or plant of your choice.

Tie the yellow ribbon around the basket, then wave your hands over the top. It will now be full of magic. Deliver the basket to the recipient so they can enjoy its healing comforts.

Kindness jar spell

By crafting a kindness jar for someone, you can gently encourage compassion to grow where unkindness has taken root, shifting their energy toward empathy and care. For best results, perform on a Friday during a new-moon phase.

YOU WILL NEED *a red pen, a strip of paper, a small jar with a lid, 1 teaspoon sugar, a bay leaf, 2 holly berries, water, a pink candle and matches.*

Using the red pen, write the name of the person who is being unkind to you on the strip of paper and place it into the jar. Add the sugar, bay leaf and holly berries, then fill the jar almost to the top with water. Put on the lid and shake the jar until the sugar dissolves, while imagining the person you've named becoming kinder. As you do so, say the following words:

'You now have a change of heart and will no longer be unkind.
You will think twice before you speak.
Your words, you will mind.
So mote it be.'

Light the pink candle and place it next to the jar. Once the candle has safely burned down, place your jar under or near to your bed for the next 28 days. You will find the other person becomes kinder to you over the next few weeks. Repeat the spell if they revert to their bad behaviour again.

Social media slumber spell

Constant screen time can drain the spirit. This spell creates peace by quieting the pull of social media, inviting rest and reconnection with the present. For best results, perform on a Friday during a new-moon phase.

YOU WILL NEED *any devices you use for social media, a black cloth, silver biodegradable glitter, a purple candle and matches.*

Gather up all the devices that you use for social media, turn them off and wrap them all in a black cloth. If you use a computer that's too large to wrap, simply cover the screen with black cloth.

Light the purple candle and say:

'It's time for slumber, it's time for sleep;
I no longer follow the herd like sheep.
I claim back my life, I claim back my time,
no longer am I tied to thine.
To slow down, to take a pause,
I am dedicated to this cause.
So be it.'

Next, take a pinch of silver glitter and throw it over the black cloth, being careful not to get any glitter on your devices themselves.

Don't touch your devices until the purple candle has safely burned down. You don't have to avoid social media now, but you will find that you naturally use it less and can reclaim some of your time and life back.

Brigid's inspiration spell

Imbolc, also known as Saint Brigid's Day, honours Brigid, the goddess of poetry, artistry and inspiration. Although she is often associated with spring, calling upon her can help spark creativity. For best results, perform during a new-moon phase.

YOU WILL NEED *painting or drawing materials, paper, a white tealight candle and matches.*

Light your candle and invite Brigid into your space, asking her to awaken your creative eye. Find an image of Brigid for inspiration and attempt to draw or paint her in any style you wish. Focus on your intention rather than perfection.

When your artwork feels complete, blow out the candle and place your creation in the space where you hope to do your creative work. This will serve as a focal point for her inspiration and guidance.

Light's return healing ritual

This spell will help you whenever you feel your light is dimmed. Imbolc, celebrated around 1 or 2 February, marks the early stirrings of spring and the gradual return of the sun's light. This ritual harnesses the seasonal energy of Imbolc to restore your inner radiance. For best results, perform it during the Imbolc period.

YOU WILL NEED *a white pillar candle, something personal to you (such as a necklace) and matches.*

Find a time when you will not be disturbed. Sit comfortably and place your personal item next to the candle. Light the candle and say the following words:

'As the dark nights draw in, the spell will begin.
So dark is the night, may you bring the light.
May the universe bring me clarity, so bright that I can't fail to see.
So mote it be.'

Allow the candle to safely burn down. Within a couple of hours, you will feel your light returning to you once again.

Imbolc confidence bloom spell

This spell uses the energy of Imbolc – renewal, light and growth – to restore and strengthen your self-confidence. For best results, cast on or around Imbolc.

YOU WILL NEED *a winter flower (such as a pansy), a pen and a hair clip.*

Place your flower on a table and think about your struggles with self-confidence. This could be anything, like not being able to make your voice heard. Now think about how you would like to feel and be. Choose a word – it could be something like 'louder', 'confident', 'fun', 'worthy' and write it on one of the petals of the flower. Choose another word for the next petal, and continue until every petal on your flower has a word representing the traits you would like to possess.

Clip the flower into your hair and say the following words:

'Brigid, I ask you to bring new life to me and bring me (say the words on your flower petals). No longer will I be small or cowed by others. So mote it be.'

Wear your flower for the rest of the day. At the end of the day, take the flower out of your hair and keep it in your favourite book. You will soon feel more confident.

Imbolc house-cleanse spray

Imbolc marks the approach of spring, making it the perfect time to refresh your home and invite in new energy. This cleansing potion fills your space with positivity, resetting your home's energy in time for the next season.

YOU WILL NEED *a spray bottle, spring water, lavender essential oil, mint essential oil, ylang ylang essential oil, lemon essential oil and rosemary essential oil.*

Fill your spray bottle with spring water then add five drops of each essential oil: lavender for peace, mint for prosperity, ylang ylang for clarity, lemon for vitality and rosemary for growth. Replace the lid and shake the potion until the oils are all mixed. Go outside and spray the front and back doors to your home as you whisper the following words:

'Cleanse, cleanse, cleanse; this I intend. Bring only peace and love to my home. Cleanse, cleanse, cleanse. The energy has now changed.'

Allow the doors to dry naturally. Next, go into every room in your home and spray the magic potion into each corner, repeating the words above. Continue until you have used up all the potion.

Your home is now cleansed and ready to welcome in the next season.

Imbolc fire spell

Imbolc is the perfect time to release what no longer serves you and welcome fresh energy into your life. This spell harnesses the element of fire to symbolically burn away the old, leaving space for growth. Perform it outside on or around Imbolc.

YOU WILL NEED *5 sparklers, sand, a cauldron or fireproof pot, matches, small pieces of paper, a pen, a red tealight candle and gloves.*

This spell is all about removing the old and inviting the new, so sit for a few minutes and write down anything or anyone in your life that you would like to move on from. Put these to one side.

Fill your cauldron or fireproof pot with sand and take it outside. Take each piece of paper and bury it in the sand, then place the red tealight on top of the sand in the centre of the cauldron. Arrange your sparklers in the sand around the candle to form a circle. Carefully light the candle first, followed by each sparkler. As the sparklers flicker into life, say the following words:

'Be gone, be gone, your time here is done.
No longer are you needed in my life, no longer do I need the strife.
Be gone, be gone, with no harm to be done.
So mote it be.'

Allow the sparklers and candle to burn away safely and leave the cauldron pot outside overnight. Dispose of the contents the following day.

Milk & honey Imbolc blessing

In Imbolc traditions, milk and honey symbolize abundance, purification and the nourishment of light and warmth returning to the world. By offering milk and honey to Brigid in this spell, you are invoking her protection and inviting abundance, luck and positive energy into your home.

YOU WILL NEED *2 teaspoons milk, 1 teaspoon honey and a jar with a lid.*

Combine the milk and honey in the jar and cover with the lid. Shake well. Take the jar outside and place it by your front door. Now say the following words:

'Dear Brigid, I bring to you an offering of milk and honey by way of gratitude for travelling by my side. May you continue to protect and encourage me to be the best I can be. So be it.'

Place an upside-down plant pot over the jar to deter any wildlife from disturbing it, and leave it outside for one night. It has been said that Brigid sometimes comes and takes the jar! If it is still there the following morning, you can wash it out, then recycle or keep it for future spells.

Heart-healing candle spell

Loss and loneliness can echo more deeply in the stillness of winter. This candle spell eases heartbreak, kindling warmth where it feels cold. For best results, perform during a new-moon phase.

YOU WILL NEED *leftover soy wax from old candles, a heatproof bowl that is large enough to sit on the rim of a saucepan, a saucepan, lavender essential oil, rose essential oil, a spoon, an old teacup, a candle wick, an old clothes peg (optional), 9 cloves and matches.*

Gather up any leftover wax you have from old candles, making sure there are no metal plates in the wax. Melt the soy wax in a heatproof bowl set over a saucepan of simmering water, making sure the bowl doesn't touch the water. Stir occasionally until the wax has fully melted.

Once the wax has melted, allow it to cool a little before adding nine drops each of the lavender and rose oils. Stir, then pour the wax into the teacup, placing the candle wick in the centre as you do so. You can use a clothes peg to hold the wick in place while the wax sets if needed. When the candle is almost set, press the cloves into the wax.

The following evening, find a time where you can sit quietly and light your candle. Release any bad feelings of hurt as its aroma fills the room.

Dating cleanse spell

Not every admirer is meant for you. This spell clears away unsuitable connections, sweeping out the energy of mismatched romances and opening space for someone truly special to enter your life. For best results, perform during a full-moon phase.

YOU WILL NEED *a black or grey pebble, a river, a white pebble and a 30cm (12in) length of leather cord.*

Hold the dark pebble in your non-dominant hand. Visualize all the unsuitable partners you've had in the past being absorbed into the pebble. Think about their unsuitable personalities and transfer those thoughts into the pebble, then say:

'Pebble, take those unsuitable people from my life and stop me from attracting the same once and for all.'

Take the dark pebble to a river and throw it over your shoulder into the water.

When you get home, take the white pebble in your dominant hand and visualize all the traits you wish to have in a new partner. Transfer this energy into the pebble. When you're happy, wrap the leather cord around the pebble as many times as you can, and tie it in a knot.

Keep this charm with you for the next 28 days to attract more suitable partners into your life.

Self-love bottle

This warm, nurturing brew calls on Aphrodite, goddess of love and beauty, to help you honour yourself. For best results, perform on a Friday.

YOU WILL NEED *dried lavender, a small rose quartz crystal, pink Himalayan salt, 3 pink rose petals, a pinch of ground cinnamon, a small glass bottle, a pink candle and matches.*

Place the dried lavender, rose quartz, salt, rose petals and cinnamon into the bottle, and blow gently into the bottle opening. Insert the pink candle into the neck of the bottle and secure by warming the wax a little to make it stay in place. Light the candle, then close your eyes and say the following words:

'I call forth the goddess Aphrodite to bring forth love and healing to me. I am loved and I am worthy. I bring back my power and love myself more and more each day. So mote it be.'

Allow the candle to safely burn down. Once the wax has cooled, your self-love bottle will be sealed with the wax. Do not reopen it.

Place it somewhere in your bedroom as a reminder that you are as worthy of love as any other person on the planet.

Attraction spell

This spell opens the way for love to enter your life, using salt to draw a special person toward you and aligning your path with theirs. For best results, perform on a Friday.

YOU WILL NEED *a red pen, sticky notes (preferably heart shaped) and salt.*

Using the red pen, write down everything you wish for in a partner on your sticky notes and place them on the floor where they won't be disturbed.

Draw a huge heart shape around the sticky notes with the salt and leave for 24 hours. Your ideal person will come into your life very soon.

Conflict resolution spell

This spell restores harmony where discord has arisen, encouraging peace between partners, friends or family. For best results, perform on a Friday.

YOU WILL NEED *an onion, a knife, a blue or black candle, matches, a white candle and a white feather.*

Chop the onion into quarters. Place one quarter in each corner of the room you spend most time in with the person with whom you're in conflict. Light the blue or black candle and repeat the following three times:

'Banish the arguments now, banish hostility, banish the hurt, so mote it be.'

Allow the candle to safely burn down and bury any remaining wax in your garden or an outside flowerpot. Wait for an hour, then light the white candle and place the feather beside it. Repeat the following three times:

'Bring peace and harmony now, bring love and excitement back to me. From here forth, only happiness will be in this relationship. So mote it be.'

Blow your wish carefully into the white feather. Allow the candle to safely burn down, then take the feather outside and throw it into the air. The universe will hear your wish. Keep the onion in your home for the next seven days, then dispose of it in the bin.

Salt & pepper money spell

This spell calls on the Hindu goddess Lakshmi, bringer of abundance. Cast during the romance season, it ensures that resources flow when most needed, whether for Valentine's, Galentine's or simply treating yourself with love. For best results, cast on a Monday or during a new-moon phase.

YOU WILL NEED *a bay leaf, a pen, a pinch each of salt and ground black pepper, and 1 metre (3 feet) of green ribbon.*

Write down how much money you need on the bay leaf. Make sure it's how much you need rather than want. Money magic works best when catering to your needs. Think about what you are going to spend the money on and how much joy it is going to bring.

Carefully sprinkle the salt and pepper on top the bay leaf. Now, take the ribbon and wrap it around the bay leaf several times, so that the leaf is completely covered. Use all the ribbon, then tie it closed to create a parcel. Hold the covered bay leaf in your dominant hand and say the following words:

'I call upon Lakshmi, the goddess of wealth, to bring forth the amount I need and to bless me with the luck of wealth in the future. So be it.'

Place the wrapped leaf in the furthest left corner of your home (looking inward from your front door). Your needs will be met within the next 28 days. When you receive the money you need, you can dispose of the leaf.

♥ Love's renewal spell

As Valentine's approaches, passion awakens. This spell reignites the spark, deepening bonds and drawing affection closer. For best results, perform on a Friday night during a full-moon phase.

YOU WILL NEED *2 red roses, a mirror that can lie flat, rose essential oil, a red candle, a red ribbon, red lipstick and matches.*

Find a time when it's quiet and you can concentrate. Place the mirror on a flat surface and write your own name and that of your partner on the mirror using the red lipstick.

Heat the bottom of the red candle to slightly melt the wax, then carefully place it in the centre of the mirror. Place the red roses on the mirror on either side of the candle, then sprinkle a few drops of rose oil on to the petals. Finish off by laying the red ribbon around the outside of the mirror.

Light the candle, close your eyes and say the following words:

'By the power of this day, I come here to say,
bring our love back again, on the count of ten.
One, two, three, four, five, six, seven, eight, nine and ten.'

The spell has now been cast. Leave the candle to safely burn down and dispose of all the spell ingredients. Clean the mirror to use another time. You will find that your partner is more romantic than ever before.

♥ Bonding love spell

This spell celebrates unity and helps bind hearts together with tenderness. For best results, perform on a Friday.

YOU WILL NEED *2 pink candles, red biodegradable glitter, a few winter rose petals, a silver pin and a tree (preferably an oak tree).*

Using the pin, carve your name into the side of one pink candle and your partner's name into the second candle. Place the candles next to each other on a clear surface, then use the glitter to draw a big red heart around the two candles. This represents the two of you being joined as one. Scatter the rose petals around the candles, then light them as you say the following words:

'These candles represent you and me,
happy together forever we shall be.'

Allow the candles to safely burn down. The following night, take the rose petals outside to a large (ideally oak) tree. Dig a small hole beside the tree and bury them in the ground. Make sure you leave the tree as you found it. You will soon notice a very happy union between you and your partner.

Gentle parting ritual

Not every love is meant to last forever. This spell eases separation with grace, helping both hearts move forward in peace. For best results, perform on a Friday evening during a full-moon phase.

YOU WILL NEED *a photograph of you and the other person, a blue candle, matches, 2 small pebbles and a bowl of water.*

Place the photograph of you and the other person underneath the candle in its holder. Light the candle with your non-dominant hand.

Hold one pebble in your right hand – this will represent you – and the other pebble in your left hand – this represents the other person. Concentrate on the pebbles. They should begin to feel warm in your palms. Mentally wish the other person well, but send them on their way as you say the following words:

'Just as these pebbles, we can now go our separate ways. I wish you no harm, and may we both find happiness in other ways. So mote it be.'

Place the pebbles into the bowl of water and leave overnight. Let the candle safely burn down. The following day, take the pebbles to a natural area and throw them in two different directions.

Self-love booster spell

In the rush of daily life, it's easy to pour energy into others and forget your own needs. This spell is a reminder to turn that care inward. For best results, perform on a Sunday night.

YOU WILL NEED *a bath, pink Himalayan salt, 6 pink or white tealight candles, matches, a bunch of your favourite flowers, your favourite drink and snacks, and a playlist of your favourite music.*

Run yourself a bath and scatter a handful of the pink salt into the water, swirling it around until it all dissolves. Arrange your tealight candles around the bath and turn off any artificial lighting. Light your candles, then take your flowers and carefully pluck the petals from them, scattering them into the water.

Prepare your favourite drink and snacks, making sure they are easily accessible when you're in the bath.

Turn on the music, sink into the bath and close your eyes. Visualize a wave of pink rising from the water and covering you. Remind yourself that you are your own best friend and will in future act accordingly. You will love yourself first before giving your love away to anyone else.

When you feel ready, drain the water, dispose of the petals and blow out the candles, promising to remind yourself every day of how special you are and that your needs come first.

★ Winter's end gratitude spell

Winter is a season of reflection, endurance and quiet lessons. It teaches us resilience, patience and the value of rest. This spell invites you to honour and thank winter for the growth it has offered, which in turn invites more blessings into your life. Perform this spell in a well-ventilated space towards the end of February in the evening.

YOU WILL NEED *an open fire or a candle, matches, paper, a pen, a sprig of dried mistletoe, natural twine and a fireproof dish.*

Light your fire or candle and sit down with some paper. Write down everything you are currently thankful for. This can be difficult, but start with the basics, such as your home or your health. Now start digging deeper. Give thanks for the people and any pets in your life, your work if you have it, the area you live in, the sun rising every morning. Keep going – every time you think you've finished, challenge yourself to write some more.

When you have spent at least half an hour writing, place the mistletoe in the centre of the paper and roll the paper into a scroll. Secure it with twine. If you have an open fire, throw the scroll into the fire. If you are using a candle, light one end of the scroll and drop it into a fireproof dish. As it burns, say:

'On this winter's night, I give thanks to my ancestors who came before me, thanks to the universe, thanks to the wisdom of this season, thanks to the gods and goddesses and thanks to life itself.'

The mistletoe inside the scroll will crackle, signalling that your thanks has been received.

SPRING

In the Wiccan calendar, spring is the season of awakening. As the days start to grow longer and the sun warms the earth, life stirs once more. After the quiet hibernation of winter, this is the time to plant intentions, nurture dreams and invite fresh energy into every part of life. With spring being all about new beginnings, it can take some time for the old days to retreat, so don't be surprised if everything goes awry for the first few weeks. This time of year is exciting because it shows us that, as with everything in life, darkness is soon replaced by light. In most of Europe, spring runs from early March through May, but wherever you live, the overarching focuses of the season remain the same: hope, expansion, fertility and joy.

Spring festivals & celebrations

Ostara *(Spring Equinox)*

Falling between 19 and 23 March, Ostara marks the balance of day and night before the scales tip as the days grow longer. It is a celebration of fertility, abundance and planting seeds, both in the soil and within ourselves.

In many traditions, this is a time to honour the youthful Maiden aspect of the Goddess and the fertile energy of the earth. Customs include decorating eggs as symbols of life, feasting and sowing the first crops of the season. Folklore tells us that hares, rabbits and other spring animals have become associated with Ostara for their prolific fertility.

For witches, Ostara is a powerful moment for spells of fertility, abundance and renewal, particularly those that focus on new beginnings and creative projects.

Beltane *(May Day)*

Celebrated on 30 April–1 May, Beltane is one of the four greater Sabbats and heralds the height of spring and the approach of summer. Traditionally, great bonfires were lit on Beltane Eve to bless livestock, fields and communities with protection and prosperity. Farmers would herd their animals between twin fires to keep them safe from harm.

Beltane is also a festival of passion, love and joy. Maypoles, flower garlands and the crowning of the May Queen are echoes of older Pagan fertility rites that honoured the union of the God and Goddess.

Like Samhain, Beltane is also said to thin the veil between worlds, making it an auspicious time for ancestor connection and spirit work. Spells of love, passion, protection and manifestation are especially potent at this time.

Spring goddesses

Brigid

Honoured at Imbolc and throughout the turning of spring, Brigid is the Celtic goddess of poetry, healing and the hearth. She represents fertility and creativity, and her fiery inspiration is often called upon during springtime.

Freyja

In Norse mythology, Freyja is a goddess of love, beauty and fertility. She governs passion, abundance and the cycles of life, making her a powerful ally for Beltane magic and love spells.

Eostre

Eostre is the Anglo-Saxon goddess of the dawn, spring and fertility, often associated with the rebirth of the land after winter. Her primary symbols are the hare and the egg: the hare embodies fertility and the dawn, while the egg symbolizes rebirth and new beginnings. Eostre's energy of vitality and new life makes her the perfect companion for Spring Equinox spells and any rituals that honour the cycles of nature.

Spring tips & recommendations

Ingredient access

Spring offers a wealth of fresh herbs and flowers to work with. Basil, mint, rosemary, sage, thyme, coriander and lavender are quick to sprout in warming soil, flourishing across Europe and the Mediterranean, though now grown worldwide. Primroses, daffodils, and cherry and hawthorn blossom are abundant in northern climates. Plant early flowers as soon as possible in spring; within a month or so, you'll be able to harvest and dry them to keep a supply for the rest of the year.

Observing nature

Make time to walk outdoors and appreciate the hopeful signs of spring's awakening: lambs in fields, blossom on trees, nests in hedgerows. Collect fallen petals or seeds to incorporate into spellwork, always with gratitude to the earth.

Crafting tools

This is the season for planting magical gardens, crafting flower garlands or weaving charms from herbs. Dedicate a patch of earth (or a window box) to growing plants for your Craft.

Best spell types for spring
Spring is ideal for spells focused on new beginnings, transitions, growth, love, fertility, passion, manifesting, prosperity, self-confidence and new ventures.

SPRING SPELLS

Seasonal shield spell

As winter fades, it's common to feel off-balance. Create a magical pouch filled with protective herbs and crystals to carry with you whenever you venture outside. For best results, craft on a Sunday.

YOU WILL NEED *a small cloth bag, a white quartz crystal, a pinch of ground cinnamon, a pinch of salt, a garlic bulb, a pinch of dried lavender, a bay leaf and a mint leaf.*

Simply place all the ingredients in the bag, one at a time, then tie it up. Carry this bag with you for protection at all times.

Fresh-start banishing spell

If there is someone who has wronged you and no amount of diplomacy seems to change things, this simple banishing spell will help remove them from your life. For best results, cast during a waning-moon phase.

YOU WILL NEED *paper, a pen, sticky tape, a mirror and a rose quartz crystal.*

Write the name of the person on the paper, then tape it to a mirror so that the name faces the mirror. Place the rose quartz below the mirror for the night. Destroy the paper the following day. The person will be safely removed from your life for good.

Lightness restored spell

When life feels heavy and your thoughts are weighing you down, this spell helps you release what no longer serves you. Perform this outside or in a well-ventilated space.

YOU WILL NEED *paper, a pen, matches and a fireproof dish.*

Write your worries or problems on the paper. Now fold it as many times as possible to shrink the worries. To remove them further, set the paper on fire while you say:

'This problem dissolves and peace is returned to me.'

Drop it into the fireproof dish to burn safely away.

New home spell

Spring is the time when many people want a fresh start and begin looking for a new living space. This happens in nature, too – baby animals are being born, and many creatures are seeking new homes, burrows and shelters. This spell taps into that same energy to help you attract a new home of your own. For best results, cast on a Thursday.

YOU WILL NEED *an old key (see note in Opportunities Spell on page 136), green paper, green ribbon, a bowl, rice, small citrine crystals, a green candle and matches.*

Place the key on the green paper, then roll up the paper into a scroll with the key inside, rolling it towards you so that you invite in positive energy. Tie the scroll with the green ribbon. Set this aside and light your green candle.

Sprinkle a handful of rice into the bowl – rice represents home. Add the citrine, which represents abundance. Place the scroll on top, then carefully lift the candle and drop a few drops of wax into the bowl to seal the deal. Say the words:

'Here's the key, the key to my new home. I send this out to the universe to find the perfect place for me. So mote it be.'

Keep the bowl and its contents somewhere safe until you are in your new home, then bury the contents somewhere in your garden (or in a flowerpot outside).

Spring broom

As the Wheel of the Year turns to spring, many witches refresh their tools to honour the new season. Creating or decorating a broom for spring is a beautiful way to align your magic with spring's energy. For best results, perform at the start of the season.

YOU WILL NEED *a broom (if you want to make one, see page 24), yellow and white ribbons, glue and a glue gun, spring decorations (such as toy chicks and eggs), fresh or dried spring flowers, jewellery or charms personal to you (optional) and a knife.*

Begin by attaching the yellow and white ribbons to the top of the broom handle, then wind the ribbons down the shaft, dabbing dots of glue along the way to keep them in place. Add any spring-related decorations and flowers to the handle and brush. You can also add personal items of jewellery, if you wish.

Finally, carve the symbol of Eostre (see reference image below) somewhere into the broom. This symbolizes welcoming in the new season.

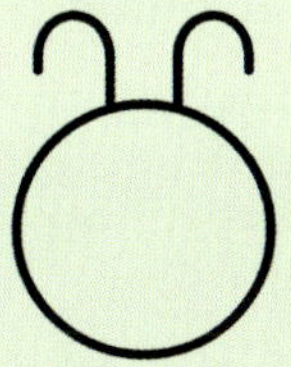

When you've finished, place the broom on the floor and, as you jump over it, say the following words:

'Eostre, I welcome you into my home as I welcome the new season.'

Your new broom is now ready to use. Always remember, if you move home, leave your broom behind and make a new one.

Spring broom reset spell

Once your spring broom is ready, follow this simple ritual to fortify your space. For best results, perform on a Monday.

YOU WILL NEED *a broom and peppermint essential oil.*

Begin at the furthest part of your home from the front door and move through your space, sweeping your broom in the air. Imagine you are sweeping anything negative out of your home. Open your front door and sweep it all out. Afterwards, sprinkle drops of peppermint oil throughout your house. This will ensure only good things enter your home in future.

Spring flower blessing jar

As the earth awakens from winter's slumber, breathtaking flowers begin to bloom aplenty, symbolizing new life and fresh opportunities. Create a flower blessing jar to capture the vibrant energy of the season and infuse your space with the magic of growth and optimism.

YOU WILL NEED *a small glass jar with a lid, a selection of spring flowers (fresh or dried), a white tealight candle, a few drops of floral essential oil (such as rose, lavender or geranium), and a small piece of ribbon in green, pink or yellow.*

Take a quiet moment outdoors, reflecting on the past season and the new beginnings you wish to welcome. Select your flowers with intention; choose blooms that represent qualities you wish to grow within yourself. Place each flower into the jar, adding a drop or two of essential oil to enhance the fragrance and energy.

Light the candle and hold the jar in your hands for a few moments, allowing your thoughts to settle on the season's energy of balance and renewal. Once the candle has safely burned away, tie the ribbon around the jar.

Keep your flower blessing jar on your spring altar (see page 75), windowsill or bedside table as a symbol of your connection to nature's cycles and your own unfolding growth.

SPRING FLOWER CORRESPONDENCES

Daffodil – for renewal and fresh beginnings
Rose – for growth, love and relationships
Lavender – for inner calm
Nettles – for psychic enhancement
Dandelion – to heal
Chamomile – to soothe and calm

Quick star protection spell

Along with taking other precautions, this quick safeguarding spell can help keep you safe when you are walking alone.

YOU WILL NEED *a black pen.*

Simply draw a small star on to the wrist of your non-dominant hand. Allow the ink to wear off, rather than washing it away.

Boundary-setting charm

Spring is the perfect time to refresh not just your surroundings, but also your personal energy. Use this spell to establish clear boundaries with friends, family or colleagues. For best results, cast this spell outside or in a well-ventilated space on a Wednesday.

YOU WILL NEED *a black pen, paper, a blue candle, matches, a fireproof dish and a few dried stinging nettles.*

With the black pen, write the word BOUNDARIES vertically in a line going down the paper. Light your blue candle and visualize setting boundaries. Repeat the word 'Boundaries' ten times. Every time you say the word, tick off one of the letters.

When you've finished, tear the paper into small pieces and place them in the fireproof dish. Add your dried nettles (careful of your hands) and hold your hand over the dish for 30 seconds. Carefully lift the candle and use the flame to set the paper alight. Allow the paper and dried nettles to burn away.

Allow your candle to safely burn down, then sprinkle the ash from the bowl across the threshold of your front door. This will send out a message to the universe that you have set your boundaries in place, and anyone who tries to cross them will have second thoughts.

Energy purge spell

It's important to regularly clear away unwanted energy from your sphere, especially after social gatherings or stressful encounters. For best results, perform during a waning-moon phase.

YOU WILL NEED *a small piece of paper, a black pen, glue, a black button, a drawing pin and a pin board.*

Write the name of the person who is affecting your energy on the paper using the black pen. Glue the black button to the head of the drawing pin, then stick it into the middle of the name on the paper and pin it to a pin board. Leave it in place for 28 days.

Home-safety ward

Spring shines a light on the domestic sphere, and sometimes that brings any 'off' energy to the forefront. Our intuition is our very own built-in alarm system. If you have a feeling that something bad is going to happen, listen to it. This quick spell will protect your home and your household.

YOU WILL NEED *2 pinches of salt and 2 pinches of ground cinnamon.*

Combine the salt and cinnamon in your hands, then walk through every room in your property, scattering the mixture as you go.

Spring heart-mending spell

This spell helps mend a broken heart, allowing you to release past hurt and make space for new love or personal growth. For best results, perform it during a new-moon phase or a Friday night.

YOU WILL NEED *a blue candle, matches, sticky tape and a bowl of soil.*

Light the blue candle using a match, then break the matchstick into two pieces. This represents your broken heart. Allow yourself time to think about what has happened and allow any hurt or angry emotions to come to the surface - have a good cry if you need to.

Now tape the matchstick pieces back together with the sticky tape. This represents you becoming whole again. Use the flame of the candle to relight the match and allow it to burn for a moment before you extinguish the matchstick in the soil and say:

'My broken heart is on the mend,
I will be free to love again.
Our love was just not meant to be,
although I hurt, I am now free.'

Take the tape off the matchstick and return the soil to nature by burying it and the matchstick pieces in the ground. Your broken heart will soon mend, and you will be free to attract someone who really deserves you.

Cherry blossom love spell

Spring is a time for romance. This spell uses cherry blossoms and the energy of Eros, the Greek god of love and sex, to deepen affection and encourage loving attention from your partner. For best results, cast on a Friday.

YOU WILL NEED *2 silver pins, a pink candle, 2 lemon balm leaves, a handful of cherry blossom and matches.*

Using the first pin, inscribe the initial of the person you love into the shaft of the pink candle. Poke the pin through the first lemon balm leaf, and then push it through the inscribed letter and into the candle. With the second pin, inscribe your initial below your lover's initial, then push the second pin into the second lemon balm leaf and then through your initial and into the candle.

Sprinkle the cherry blossom around the base of the candle, then light the candle. Say the following words:

'Eros, I call upon you to bring forth feelings of love to me, from thee. I call upon your power, on this day, to heal my heart and remind others how loveable I am. This is my request to you; so mote it be.'

Allow the candle to safely burn down, then dispose of the spell ingredients. You will find that your lover will become more attentive to you.

Unbinding obstacles spell

When progress feels slow and setbacks keep stopping you from fully stepping into spring's fast-paced rhythm, it may be a sign of energetic blockages. This simple spell helps clear obstacles from your path, restoring flow to your life. For best results, perform during a new-moon phase.

YOU WILL NEED *a cinnamon stick, 3 cloves, a white tealight candle and matches.*

Push the cloves into the top of the cinnamon stick. Light your candle, then, using the candle flame, light the cinnamon stick. Walk through every room in your home and waft the smoke from the cinnamon stick around. Carefully waft the smoke around yourself as well. Blockages will soon be removed from your life. When you're finished, extinguish the cinnamon stick and dispose of it safely.

Salt protection spell

This simple protective spell will help fortify your home from negative energies. Perform any time you notice your home feels less harmonious.

YOU WILL NEED *a shot glass, salt and 3 bay leaves.*

Simply fill your shot glass with salt, then add the bay leaves. Place on a windowsill. This will prevent anything negative coming into your house. Refresh once a month.

Reflected curse reversal

If you suspect that someone has sent you negative energy, this quick spell can help return that energy to its source.

YOU WILL NEED *a small mirror.*

Sit in a chair with the mirror in front of you. Look into it so that you can see whatever is behind you reflected.

Say:

'Mighty Eostre, return this curse to the source. May you be my messenger here and now.'

Turn the mirror face down and then walk away.

Spring travel safety charm

As the weather turns for the better, you may wish to get on the road. This charm protects you on your journeys.

YOU WILL NEED *9 silver paperclips, a selection of small spring flowers (such as daisies and buttercups) and red string.*

To begin, link the paperclips together so that they form a long line. Next, thread the red string through all the paperclips, then tie with a knot at the top and bottom. Take your spring flowers and thread them into the paperclips, so that you have a long line of flowers on the paperclip chain.

To bless the chain, lay it on a flat surface and hover your hand, palm downwards, over the chain. Repeat the following nine times:

'I bless this chain by the power of nine,
protection and safety will be mine.
So mote it be.'

Hang your blessed charm somewhere in your car, and it will protect you from harm while driving. Replace when the flowers have died.

Energy circle reset spell

Our energy can wane when we spend too much time in draining environments. This ritual circle helps you recharge your energy. For best results, cast it on a Sunday evening or during a new-moon phase.

YOU WILL NEED *a bunch of spring flowers, salt, paper, a cushion, meditation music, 3 tealight candles and matches.*

Arrange the flowers in a circle large enough for you to sit in, trying to make sure it is unbroken. Within the flower circle, draw a circle of salt. Draw a pentagram (a five-pointed star within a circle, see page 124) on the paper and place it in the centre of the salt circle. Place the cushion on top of it.

Put on your favourite meditation music, then carefully step into the circle with your candles and matches. Sit on the cushion with your legs crossed. Light the candles and say:

'In the name of the triple goddess, the Maiden, the Mother and the Crone, I ask that you bring inner peace back to me and reject the energy vampires. Here I sit and wait for a sign that all is back in harmony and that all is well again.'

Remain in the circle until you feel re-energized and have a sense that the goddesses have answered your call. When you're happy, you can blow out the candles, exit the circle and clean it up.

Garden guardian spell

With spring's awakening, your garden becomes a sacred space in need of nurturing and shielding. For best results, cast this spell at sunrise to protect your garden from negative energies or unwanted intrusions.

YOU WILL NEED *wildflower seeds.*

Walk around the perimeter of your garden three times, sprinkling the wildflower seeds and saying:

'Spirits of nature, protect this sacred space. Bless the earth I tread upon. Let peace and beauty reside.'

Water the seeds regularly.

Spring renewal egg spell

Eggs symbolize rebirth and renewal. This simple spell uses an egg to absorb negativity, stagnant energy or physical and emotional discomfort. Perform it whenever you feel depleted to give yourself a little refresh.

YOU WILL NEED *a chicken egg.*

Just before you go to bed, take an egg and gently roll it across your forehead, or along the area where you are in pain. Imagine it absorbing any disease or pain, mental or physical. Place the egg under your bed, and bury it the following day.

Spring laundry spell

Spring is the perfect time to refresh your home and yourself through your everyday chores. With this spell, you will turn doing your laundry into a magical ritual that infuses your clothes with positive energy and spring magic.

YOU WILL NEED *laundry ready for washing and your favourite essential oils (I like to use a lavender, rosemary and lemon).*

Add your regular detergent to the washing machine, along with 3–9 drops of your chosen essential oils. Put on your wash as normal.

Once washed, hang your laundry outside to dry in the spring sunshine. Imagine the warmth of the sun charging your clothing with vibrant energy. Each time you wear these freshly washed items, carry with you the intention that your day is filled with positivity.

Spring moon bath ritual

Bathe in the gentle energy of the moon to refresh your spirit and align with the season's cycles. Making this a monthly ritual is ideal, and you can tailor it to your intention: a waning moon to release unwanted energies, or a new or full moon to manifest your desires.

YOU WILL NEED *a bath, a full jar of moon water (see page 18), lavender essential oil, a bath tea bag (available at health stores), a rose quartz crystal, a white quartz crystal, a white candle and matches.*

Fill a bath with warm water, then pour in the moon water. Add a few drops of the lavender oil and the tea bag. Place the crystals on the side of the bath. Extinguish any artificial lighting, then light your candle, stir the water to disperse the oil and step into the bath. As you relax in the water, visualize the power of the moon water cleansing and energizing your soul.

Stay in the bath for as long as you like, enjoying the magical process. The longer you lie there, the more positive cleansing energy will be manifested. If you are wishing for a change in your life, focus on how you will feel when it happens. Dry yourself off and then relax for the evening.

Jewellery energy recharge

Cleanse the energy of your crystals, pendants and enchanted jewellery with this simple ritual. This is especially important for divination tools, and any items that you are bringing into your home for the first time, particularly second-hand pieces. This will ensure they carry only your intended vibration.

YOU WILL NEED *jewellery or crystals for cleansing, a bowl, water and salt.*

Place your chosen items in the bowl and fill it with a salt-water solution (1 teaspoon salt per 100ml/3½fl oz water). Leave for 30 minutes to cleanse the items of residual or negative energy.

Happy home spring charm

Spring is the perfect time to restore balance in your home. This spell calls upon Athena, the warrior goddess of order and peace, to clear tension, invite positive energy and create a nurturing environment for everyone under your roof. For best results, cast on a Thursday.

YOU WILL NEED *a bowl, salt, 1 teaspoon cinnamon, a basil leaf, an onion, a knife, a blue candle, a white candle, a green candle, matches and blue ribbon.*

Fill the bowl with salt, then add the cinnamon and basil leaf. Cut the onion in half and cover both halves with the salt. Light the candles in the following order: blue, green and white. Now say the following words:

'Athena, warrior goddess of order and peace, hear my cry and take hold of this situation. Banish any negativity from the home, so that all feels safe and secure again. May you protect me always and release positive energy, healing and peace. So mote it be.'

Wait for the candles to safely burn down, then move through every room in your home, sprinkling a little salt and cinnamon in each one. Go outside and sprinkle the mixture by your front door. Finally, place the basil leaf between the two onion halves, then use the blue ribbon to tie the halves together. Place this under your bed for 14 days. Your home will now become a happy haven.

Remote healing spell

This remote healing spell allows you to send supportive, restorative energy to someone in need, even from a distance.

YOU WILL NEED *white paper, scissors, a red pen, a white candle, matches and a green pen.*

Take your paper and cut out the shape of a person (like a paper doll). With the red pen, draw a heart to mark the area on the paper person's body where the real person's pain is. Light your candle and say the following prayer:

'I ask Brigid that you heal (name) from the pain they suffer. May it ease day by day until it disappears altogether. I ask that you mend this problem and take it away, so that it may never return for another day.'

Take your green pen and draw a thick circle around the red heart you made earlier, then carefully place the paper figure underneath the candle, visualizing healing energy being sent towards the person. Allow the candle to safely burn away, then dispose of the paper figure. The person you are healing should begin to feel better very soon.

Note: This is not an alternative to seeking medical help.

★ Astrological New Year blessing

In astrology, the true new year begins not in January, but when the sun enters Aries, the first sign of the zodiac. This marks a cosmic reset, when the energy of rebirth and possibility flows. It's the perfect time to reflect and set fresh intentions. Choose your sun sign below and perform the ritual that aligns with your energy to invite blessings into your new astrological year.

Aries – *Draw the symbol of the ram on the palm of your dominant hand with a washable pen. Press your palms together and visualize stepping confidently into the year ahead, full of strength and purpose.*

Taurus – *Fill a china cup with water and add a few fresh spring flowers. Leave the cup outside overnight to absorb earth's blessings and invite abundance into your coming year.*

Gemini – *To honour your dual nature, light one black and one white tealight candle side by side, embracing all aspects of yourself and the balance they bring.*

Cancer – *Visit a beach or body of water and find a shell or stone. Write a single heartfelt wish upon it, then offer it back to the water, trusting that the tides will carry your desire to fruition.*

Leo – *As a sign of courage, write down a challenge or worry on a piece of paper. Burn it in a fireproof dish or cauldron to release fear and ignite strength.*

Virgo – *Tap into your natural intuition by filling a bowl with water and gazing softly into its surface. Ask the universe to reveal a symbol or message about your year ahead.*

Libra – *To call in fairness and balance, carry the Justice Tarot card with you for 14 days. As you do, clarity and resolution will begin to unfold.*

Scorpio – *To nurture emotional depth and self-love, sleep with a rose quartz under your pillow for 28 nights, allowing its energy to open your heart gently.*

Sagittarius – *Draw an arrow on a dried bay leaf and tuck it inside your shoe. Each step you take will move you closer to manifesting your dreams.*

Capricorn – *Sit in quiet meditation with a crystal that calls to you. Focus on releasing old energy and grounding into renewed strength and ambition for the year ahead.*

Aquarius – *Pour a glass of water and place it on your windowsill under the full moon. Drink it the next morning to invite luck, inspiration and forward movement into your life.*

Pisces – *Embrace your connection to water by swimming in an outdoor pool, river or sea. As you float, imagine your worries washing away and insight flowing in.*

Personal power restoration spell

Spring is the season of renewal, making it the perfect time to reclaim your personal power. This spell helps restore your confidence, inner strength and sense of self, especially if others have tried to diminish you through jealousy or fear. For best results, perform during a new-moon phase.

YOU WILL NEED *a piece of black card and a silver pen.*

Find a time when you can sit quietly at a desk or table. Take your piece of black card and write the following words with the silver pen:

'Today I call back my power. I call back my energy. I cut ties with toxicity and poison, and anyone or anything that intentionally causes me harm. I cast aside the evil eye of others, so that it is reflected back. I cast aside any ill-will directed towards me. I am now protected from the sinful ways of others. As it is so, so mote it be.'

Read these words out loud three times, then fold the card three times. Keep it with you, and whenever you feel someone is trying to take your power from you, read it another three times.

Earth healing ritual

Spring invites us to reconnect with the restorative power of nature to remind ourselves of her enduring resilience through winter. This ritual uses the earth's energy to cleanse and rejuvenate your body, mind and spirit. Perform it whenever you feel the need for healing.

YOU WILL NEED *a handful of dried herbs, a clear quartz crystal and a bowl of water.*

Sit outside on the ground to connect with Mother Earth. Place the herbs and quartz into the bowl of water. Dip your fingers into the water and pat your face with it, visualizing the natural energy healing you. When you are happy, pour the water on the ground, and carry the crystal in your pocket for at least 28 days.

Cleansing bell spell

Sound is known to energetically clear stagnant energy. If you have felt a shift in your living space, use this simple spell to clear the atmosphere.

YOU WILL NEED *a bell.*

Simply walk through your home while sounding the bell to reset the atmosphere and invite positivity.

★ Sun awakening spell

It is time to harness the energy of the sun to awaken your inner light. This spell encourages you to take a longer view of your year and contemplate your summer goals now, growing these desires through spring via sunflower seeds. For best results, begin this spell between April and May.

YOU WILL NEED *an orange pen, a couple of stones, a flowerpot, compost, sunflower seeds, water, garden netting and plant feed.*

Think of a few simple words that describe what you wish your summer to be like. Using your orange pen, write these words on the stones. Place the stones into the bottom of the flowerpot, where they will act as drainage. Fill the pot two-thirds full with compost, then add a couple of sunflower seeds. Cover with more compost. Finally, water the soil, then cover the top of the pot with some netting – birds love sunflower seeds, so this will protect them while they grow.

Sunflowers require a lot of water, so make sure you water the pot every day and add some plant feed every fortnight. As your seeds begin to sprout, you can transfer them into individual pots if you want them to grow bigger.

Your sunflowers will bloom around mid-May and will last until the autumn. By this time, your summer wishes should have come to fruition. When the flowers have come to the end of their lives, you can collect the seeds for use in the kitchen – or for repeating the spell next year.

Ostara doll blessing

Mark Ostara (the Spring Equinox) with a ritual that celebrates revitalization, growth and good fortune. This spell uses a small rosemary doll symbolizing the spirit of Ostara to invite luck into your home. For best results, perform it during Ostara.

YOU WILL NEED *5 sprigs of rosemary, green ribbon, scissors, green paper, a green pen and glue.*

Form the rosemary sprigs into the shape of a doll: two legs, two arms and a torso. Use the ribbon to tie the sprigs together. Next, cut out a small circle from the green paper and use your green pen to draw a little face on it. Stick the face on to your rosemary dolly. When you're happy with your creation, stand her in front of you and repeat the following words:

'Lucky Rose, I give you a home, warmth and comfort in return for your luck and good fortune. Help me in my quest for good luck, and return any bad luck to its original source. So mote it be.'

Place your rosemary doll somewhere where you will see her every day. She will bring you lots of luck in the future.

Springtime altar

Honour the energy of spring to invite abundance, growth and joy into your life by creating a dedicated seasonal altar. Collect seasonal flora and other personal items that reflect the season's energy to help you focus your springtime intentions. For best results, craft your altar in early March.

YOU WILL NEED *a bare branch with lots of twigs on it, a flower pot, stones, frankincense essential oil, ribbons in various colours, a few bells, any spare jewellery you may have, a yellow or orange pen, yellow or orange sticky notes and fresh spring flowers.*

Secure the branch in your pot with stones so that it won't fall over. Sprinkle a few drops of frankincense oil over the branch, then decorate it with the ribbon, bells and any jewellery items you may have.

Using the orange or yellow pen, write down anything that you want to manifest on the sticky notes, writing one manifestation per note. Fold each note around a twig so that it sticks to itself. Finally, decorate the base of the tree with your spring flowers (replace these when they begin to wither).

This branch can serve as the main decoration on your springtime altar, and it will help you to manifest what you want for the next few months.

Egg divination spell

Eggs symbolize the rebirth, but they can also serve as powerful divination tools. Also known as Oomancy, egg divination was practised in ancient Greece and Rome, where it was believed that an egg could reveal a person's future. Many cultures have their own variations on this practice, but the following method draws on the Greek tradition. Perform this spell whenever you are seeking clarity or insight.

YOU WILL NEED *a chicken or duck egg, a cup and a bowl of hot water.*

In your mind, ask the goddess Eostre to guide you to the answer you need. Take the egg and roll it over your forearms so that the egg can feel the energy of your question. Carefully break the egg, then hold it over a cup and separate the yolk from the white, so that you are left with the egg white in the cup.

Close your eyes and drop the egg white into the bowl of hot water. When it meets the hot water, the egg white will change shape, and this is when your intuition comes into play. Look into the water and see what shape the egg white has created. For example, if it forms a ring, you could take this to mean that a wedding is on the horizon.

With practice, you will be able to recognize different shapes and interpret their meanings.

Spring refresh daffodil spell

Springtime is the moment to shed what no longer serves you. This spell helps you release the past to make space for growth, joy and fresh beginnings. For best results, cast it during Ostara or on a Sunday morning.

YOU WILL NEED *a bunch of daffodils (or other yellow flowers), a vase, water, a yellow ribbon, a yellow candle, matches, a yellow pen and a yellow sticky note.*

Take some time to arrange your flowers in a vase of water, then tie the yellow ribbon around the vase. Next, light the candle and look into the flame. Visualize its glow surrounding and energizing you with positive feelings. Don't think about the past. It's time to think about your future and what it is that you want in your life now.

Using the yellow pen, write the following words on the yellow sticky note:

'Here forthwith I claim my fresh start and no longer dwell on the past. This is my wish, so be it.'

Allow the candle to safely burn down, then roll the sticky note into a scroll so that it sticks to itself, and slip it behind the ribbon on the vase. You will now feel more positive about your future.

Ostara crown ritual

Celebrate the vibrant energy of Ostara by creating a crown that embodies spring's renewal, abundance and rebirth. Make this crown in the days leading up to the Spring Equinox.

YOU WILL NEED *a tape measure, jewellery wire, wire cutters, natural twine, scissors, a glue gun and glue, a selection of spring flowers and greenery (such as ivy), mint leaves, bay leaves, twigs, a white candle and matches.*

Start by measuring the crown of your head with the tape measure, then use this as a guide to cut a length of jewellery wire for your crown. Add 5cm (2in) to the length to enable you to fasten it in a circle. Place it on your head to check that it fits securely.

Wind the twine tightly around the wire frame and glue in place. Now you can insert your flowers, ivy, mint and bay leaves and twigs into the garden twine. Glue them in place to secure them.

When you're happy with your decorations, lay the crown on a flat surface and place the white candle in the centre and light it. This will bless your crown. Allow the candle to safely burn away before wearing the crown.

Wear this crown whenever you are casting spring spells to enhance their seasonal power.

♥ Blooming heart spell

Now is the time for blossoms and blossoming connections. If your heart is ready to open to love, this spell invites romance into your life. For best results, cast on a Friday to align with Venus's romantic influence.

YOU WILL NEED *dried mixed herbs, a small bowl, rose essential oil, a pink candle, matches and a heart-shaped locket.*

Place a pinch of dried herbs in the bowl, then add three drops of rose oil. Allow the herbs and oil to dry. Light your pink candle and say the following words:

'I call upon Freyja, goddess of love, to serve me here.
I'm ready again, I feel you near.
I'm open now to find new love.
I call upon you from above.
To go out and find the one for me,
so that our souls are joined in harmony.
So mote it be.'

As the candle burns down, take the dried herbs and pop them into your locket, but don't close the locket until the candle has safely burned away. Once it has, snap the locket shut and the spell is sealed.

You will begin to notice how many admirers are sent your way. They may be people whom you already know but are suddenly seeing in a new light.

♥ Clay love spell

Clay is a useful magical tool in witchcraft, and can be used to craft charms, talismans, cauldrons and other objects imbued with earth's powerful energy. This spell shapes love into a tangible form, inviting genuine affection into your life. For best results, cast it on a Friday or during a full-moon phase.

YOU WILL NEED *air-dry modelling clay, a rolling pin, a knife or heart-shaped cookie cutter, a pencil, dried rosemary, dried lavender, red paint or nail varnish and a brush, and a red ribbon.*

Knead your clay so that it becomes soft and pliable. As you do so, visualize the type of person you would like as a partner. What are their traits? Are they kind, caring and lots of fun?

Roll out the clay until it's about 5mm (¼in) thick. Cut the clay into a heart shape using either a knife or a cookie cutter. Push the point of a pencil into the top of the heart to make a hole. Take a few bits of dried rosemary and lavender and push them into the clay while it's still soft. All the while, keep visualizing who your new partner will be.

Allow your clay heart to dry in a warm place overnight. When your heart is completely dry, you can paint it with the red paint or nail varnish. Paint both the front and back. Once it's dry, thread the red ribbon through the hole you made.

Hang this over your bed and visualize sending your love out to the universe to attract your perfect partner.

Ostara career blessing

This spell harnesses the season's energy of growth and opportunity to help your business or career thrive. For best results, cast it during Ostara.

YOU WILL NEED *a sheet of letterhead paper or a business card (or something that represents your business or career), a green pen, a green candle, a small mint plant, 5 silver coins and matches.*

Take your paper or business card and on it use the green pen to write:

'My business/career flourishes.'

Place the green candle on top of the paper. Pick five leaves from the mint plant and arrange them around the candle. Place a silver coin on top of each mint leaf and light the candle. Allow the candle to safely burn down, then place the silver coins and mint leaves on top of the earth of your mint plant. Recycle the sheet of paper and wait until the Spring Equinox has passed before removing the coins and leaves from the plant pot. Keep these in your purse.

Water your mint plant. As it grows, so your business or career will flourish.

Basil fertility spell

For centuries, basil has been used to encourage fertility, so if you're thinking of conceiving a baby, spring is the ideal time to plant basil in your home and garden. As the plant grows, you can use the leaves in various ways to invite fertility, or to bring new ideas and projects to life.

YOU WILL NEED *basil.*

It's very simple: just find ways to intentionally bring basil into your life and daily activities. You can add fresh basil to your meals, carry a few leaves around in a small pouch and hang fragrant bunches over your bed, replacing them once they start to wilt.

Spring Solstice decorating two ways

Part one:
Solstice egg painting

This spell uses eggs – a symbol of life and rebirth – to welcome the energy of spring into your home. For best results, cast it during Ostara.

YOU WILL NEED 6 *chicken or duck eggs, a sewing needle, a bowl, paint (various colours), pens (various colours), glue, biodegradable glitter and any other decorations you like, and thin ribbon.*

First, extract the egg's contents from the shells. You can do this by using the needle to carefully pierce a hole in the top and bottom of each egg, then gently blowing into the top hole. This will make the egg inside come out at the bottom. Use a bowl to catch the contents to make a magical omelette later.

Do this with each egg and allow the shells to dry on a sunny windowsill. When they are dry, decorate them using paint, pens, glitter and any other decorations you like. However you decorate the shells, make sure they are personal to you and linked to the season of spring.

When you're happy with your shells, carefully thread a piece of ribbon through both holes in each shell and tie a knot to secure it at the bottom. You can now hang your decorated eggshells around your home as you celebrate the sun returning.

Part two:
Solstice egg dyeing

This egg dyeing spell harnesses the power of the Berkano rune – the rune of rebirth, spring, renewal and growth. For best results, cast this spell during Ostara.

YOU WILL NEED 6 *chicken or duck eggs, a sewing needle, a bowl, a pot of boiling water, natural dyes (beetroot, blueberries, onion skin or red cabbage), white ribbon, a needle with a large eye, paper towels and a silver pen or marker.*

First, extract the egg's contents from the shells (see Solstice Egg Painting). Prepare your dyes by simmering your chosen ingredients in separate pots of water. Once cooled slightly, place an eggshell in each dye bath and leave it to absorb the colour for around ten minutes. Natural dyes produce soft, organic shades: beetroot gives pink tones, blueberries yield blue, onion skins a warm amber and red cabbage a gentle violet. Allow each shell to dry on a paper towel.

When dry, thread a length of white ribbon through the shells using a needle and secure it with a small knot at the base. With the silver pen, draw the Berkano rune (see reference image below) on to each shell.

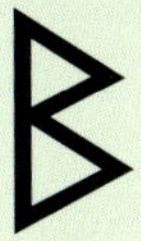

Hang your finished eggs on a branch, Ostara tree, or in a bright window.

Soulmate charm spell

Fertile springtime energies awaken the promise of love. This spell helps open your heart to attract a soulmate. For best results, perform on a Friday or during a new-moon phase.

YOU WILL NEED *2 pink candles, matches, 60cm (24in) pink ribbon, 60cm (24in) white ribbon, 60cm (24in) red ribbon, a few rose petals (fresh or dried), a strand of your hair and a white envelope.*

Light the candles, then tie all three lengths of ribbon together with one knot at the top, so that you have three tails hanging down. Braid the ribbons together. As you do so, say the following:

'Our hearts and lives entwine together,
the person I meet will be forever,
they with me and me with them,
let this spell of love begin.'

Once you've braided the ribbon, tie the ends together to create a circle. Carefully place this ribbon circle over the two candles.

Finally, place the ribbon, rose petals and a strand of your hair into the envelope. Just before the candles have safely burned away, seal the envelope with a few drops of wax. Carry your envelope in your purse until the next new moon.

Magical spring foot soak

Spring is a season of awakening, when energy stirs and hope blossoms. This relaxing bathing ritual helps refresh your body and spirit. For best results, perform on a calm Sunday evening.

YOU WILL NEED *a large bowl of cold spring water, lavender essential oil, rose essential oil, peppermint essential oil, a towel, a white tealight candle and matches.*

Find a time when you can relax alone. Fill your large bowl with the cold spring water (the cold water will wake up your circulation). Add five drops of each essential oil, then swirl the water around.

As you do, say the following words:

'Magic water in my bowl, I ask that you now fill my soul.
Through the soles of my feet, my heart skips a beat,
as you bring a spring to my step, giving me energy to forge ahead.
So mote it be.'

Light your candle and place your feet in the bowl and focus on the flame. It's best to keep your feet in the water for at least three minutes.

When you're ready, dry your feet on a towel and extinguish the candle for use again. Dispose of the water outside, not down the sink.

★ Ostara future blessing

Spring is the perfect season to manifest for your future. This spell harnesses the energy of Ostara to help you clarify your goals and send them out into the universe. For best results, cast during the Ostara celebration.

YOU WILL NEED *a tree, yellow ribbon, red or pink ribbon, green ribbon, blue ribbon, scissors and a pen.*

Spend some time thinking about what you would like your future to look like. Break it down into four different areas: your home life, your love life, your finances and your career.

When you're happy with what you want, cut several pieces of each colour of ribbon, making each about 12cm (5in) long. On each of the yellow ribbons, write down one thing you want in your home life. Do the same with the other colours: red or pink is for your love life, green is for your future finances and blue is for your career.

Take all the ribbons outside and tie them to your favourite tree to send your wishes to the universe.

★ Intentional magic seeds

Spring is the season of sprouts, buds and blossoms, making it the perfect time to plant your intentions alongside nature. Cast this spell on any bright spring morning.

YOU WILL NEED *seeds of your choice, plant pots, compost and water.*

Read the instructions on how to plant the seeds of your choice, but before you plant them, whisper your intentions or desires to the seeds. Fill your plant pots with compost and plant the seeds. Water them and care for them. As the seeds germinate and grow, so will the wishes you requested.

Magical garden pots

Spring is the perfect time to prepare your garden (or even a few window pots). As the earth awakens, this spell blesses your plants with positive energy, helping everything you grow to thrive.

YOU WILL NEED *a selection of terracotta pots in different sizes and a white enamel paint pen.*

Before planting anything new, hold each pot in your hands and take a few deep breaths, visualizing white light filling the clay with protective and nurturing energy. Using your white pen, draw protective symbols around the sides and base of each pot, such as a pentagram, crescent moon, spiral or sun.

Springtime glow spell

Eggs symbolize vitality, and their utility extends beyond the egg itself to the water used in cooking them.

YOU WILL NEED *an egg, a pen, a saucepan, water and a glass bowl.*

Write the name Eostre (the goddess associated with spring) on the shell of your egg, then fill a saucepan with water and boil the egg until it's cooked to your liking. When the egg is ready, eat it as normal, but don't drain the water. Allow the water to cool, then decant it into a glass bowl. When you go to bed that evening, wash your face with the egg water. Your skin will look radiant the following day.

Spring confidence charm

This empowering spell helps you rediscover your self-belief. For best results, cast on a Wednesday.

YOU WILL NEED *a mirror, a yellow or gold candle, matches, paper, a pen and a small bag or pouch.*

Find a time when you can be undisturbed. Place your candle in front of the mirror and light it. Take a few deep breaths and think about what you would say to a loved one who is lacking in confidence right now. Write down a few sentences, but use 'I' rather than 'you', for example: 'I am more than capable of public speaking.'

Look through the candle into the mirror and read your words aloud to your reflection. Feel the warmth of the flame encouraging you that you are confident and that you can achieve anything you want in life.

When you're feeling happier, fold the paper into three and place it in your pouch or bag. Allow the candle to safely burn down. Carry your confidence pouch with you and reread your words whenever you are feeling less than.

Rejuvenating spring bath

Spring is the perfect time for a refresh, and this ritual bath helps you wash away stagnant energy. Infused with flowers, oils and crystals, this bath will leave you feeling cleansed and uplifted.

YOU WILL NEED *a large empty jar with lid (a mason jar is ideal), pink Himalayan salt, lavender essential oil, rose essential oil, jasmine essential oil, chamomile essential oil, a wand, a small clear quartz crystal, a small rose quartz crystal, a sprig of lavender, a few rose petals, a bathtub, a white candle and matches.*

Start by filling your jar two-thirds full with Himalayan salt, then add six drops of each of the essential oils. Use your wand (or a natural stick) to mix the oils into the salt. Add the two crystals and stir again. Finally, add the sprig of lavender and the rose petals. Stir again and say:

'With this wand I create a magical cleanse. Mix, mix, mix this magical blend. What is meant for me will come to me. What is not, will float away. I add this magic to my bath and wait for glorious days. So mote it be.'

Close the lid on the jar and leave it on a windowsill overnight to gain power. Whenever you feel like a magical bath, fill a tub with warm water, light the white candle and pour a little of your magical blend into the bath. Agitate the water to disperse the blend before entering the bath. You will feel revitalized and refreshed afterwards.

Spring's stillness meditation

Spring awakens the hum of life all around us. This simple ritual invites you to pause and breathe, letting nature's effortless rhythm remind you how to live in the present moment. Perform this meditation every time you feel overwhelmed or burdened.

YOU WILL NEED *a quiet outdoor spot where you can sit comfortably.*

Find a place where you can observe the signs of spring: flowers opening, bees humming, birdsong or even a gentle breeze. Sit quietly for at least 20 minutes. As you watch, breathe deeply and let your thoughts settle.

With every breath, imagine your worries dissolving into the air. If you see a butterfly, bee or bird, take it as a blessing - a reminder that new life is all around you.

When you feel lighter, whisper:

***'With earth I heal, with spring I grow,
My spirit clears, my heart will glow.'***

Rain magic growth spell

Spring showers nourish the earth, nurturing seeds and coaxing plants into bloom. Rainwater is one of the purest forms of water and is perfect for many spells, so whenever you hear that a rain shower is coming, get out and collect as much of it as you can.

YOU WILL NEED *a clean bucket or large container, a rainy day or night, a few bottles or jars with lids and a large, clean bowl.*

Leave a large container out in the rain, then decant it into some clean jars or bottles and store in a dark cupboard. Ideally during a new-moon phase, take a stored jar or bottle and pour the contents into a bowl. Before bed, wash your face and hands with the rainwater and pat them dry. The purity of the water will encourage growth in your life. You can also use rainwater to rinse your hair after shampooing. It will leave it silky soft and will promote personal development.

Bay leaf wish spell

Wind is a powerful messenger, and you can use its power to release your manifestations into the world. For best results, perform this ritual on a windy day.

YOU WILL NEED *a bay leaf, a pen and a windy day.*

Think carefully about the wish you want Mother Nature to grant you, then write it down on your bay leaf. When it's windy outside, throw the bay leaf up into the air to let the wind carry your wish to the universe.

Spring abundance spell

Spring is the perfect time to align yourself with the universe's flow of prosperity. This abundance spell helps you attract wealth, opportunities and resources. For best results, cast it during a full-moon phase.

YOU WILL NEED *a pen, green paper, 3 mint leaves, a citrine crystal, an aquamarine crystal, natural twine and peppermint essential oil.*

Draw your currency symbol (such as £, $ or €) in the centre of the green paper, then place the mint leaves on top of it. Next, place both crystals on top of the mint leaves. Now fold the corners of the paper into each other to hold everything in place. Secure with the garden twine to create a small green parcel.

Sprinkle three drops of peppermint oil on to your parcel and say the following words:

'With this money parcel, I encourage wealth, abundance and prosperity to me. By the powers of the earth, I have more than enough. So mote it be.'

Place your money parcel in the furthest left corner of the room you that you spend most time in your home (if you were looking into your home from your front door). This is the prosperity area of your home. Leave the parcel there until the next full moon.

Spring essence room spray

This spell uses the natural fragrance of seasonal flowers to clear stagnant energy and invite new vibrations into your space. For best results, cast during a new-moon phase.

YOU WILL NEED *a selection of spring flowers, a jug, a spoon, hot water, a strainer, a funnel and a small spray bottle.*

Pick your flowers, then place them in a jug. Using the back of a spoon, crush the flowers to extract their natural fragrance and oils. Add hot water to the jug and stir in a clockwise direction. Leave the flowers to steep for around ten minutes.

The water should now smell floral. Carefully strain the flower water into your spray bottle with the help of a strainer and funnel. Leave the solution to cool.

Once cool, go through every room in your home and spray the magical flower spray into the air a few times. Visualize the spray taking away any negative or stagnant energy. Repeat once a week until you run out of magical spray, then make another batch.

★ Spring dream board

While January is widely considered the start of the calendar year, in Wiccan and Pagan traditions, spring has always marked the beginning of the spiritual year. This makes it the perfect time to set intentions for the months ahead. Creating a dream board is a fun and visual way to manifest your desires. Perform this ritual anytime between March and May.

YOU WILL NEED *a large piece of card or posterboard, 4 bay leaves, sticky tape, a photo of yourself, coloured pens, magazines, scissors, glue and biodegradable glitter in various colours.*

Find a time when you will not be disturbed, and gather up all your materials in one place, on a table or at a desk. Set your magical intention by taping one bay leaf to each corner of your piece of card or posterboard. Bay is the natural symbol of success.

Stick the photo of yourself in the centre of the card, then draw lots of arrows out from your picture. Have a flick through your magazines for words or images that sum up who you want to be and what you want to achieve in the coming year. Once you find an image or a word that resonates with you, cut it out and stick it at the end of an arrow. When you're happy, finish off the magic by adding lots of glitter. Pin up your dream board somewhere where you will see it every day.

★ Deity gratitude offering

Gratitude is one of the most powerful things we can do to maintain a happy life. This spell helps you honour the goddesses who guide and protect us, inviting their blessings into your life.

YOU WILL NEED *a white candle, matches, a white quartz crystal, spring flowers and natural twine.*

Find a place where you can set up an altar that won't be disturbed. Light your candle and place the crystal in front of it. Arrange the flowers into a bouquet and tie them with the twine. Place the bouquet in front of the crystal. Say the following words:

'To all the goddesses, from Morrigan to Brigid, I give this spring offering to you as a way of thanks for protecting and helping me on this magical journey we call life. I bless and thank you all. I am open to your guidance and embrace you travelling with me throughout life. Blessed and thanked be.'

Leave the altar in place until the candle has safely burned away, then take the bouquet outside somewhere and throw it over your shoulder. Sleep with the crystal under your pillow that night. You may receive a visit from one of your ancestorial guides or a goddess.

Quick housework blessing

Why not bring a little magic into your spring-cleaning routine? This simple spell uses herbs to bless your home while you tidy.

YOU WILL NEED *a hessian pouch, 1 teaspoon dried rosemary, 1 teaspoon dried lavender, 1 teaspoon dried mint and a vacuum cleaner.*

Place all the dried herbs in the pouch and pull the drawstrings to close it. Open your vacuum cleaner and place the pouch where the filter sits. Every time you vacuum your home, it will be magically blessed. Replace the pouch after a few weeks of use.

Intentions brew spell

Tea is more than just a comforting drink; it's a vessel for magic. You can use a daily ritual like tea-drinking to set intentions, whether you want to manifest new opportunities or release what no longer serves you. Perform this ritual as often as you like.

YOU WILL NEED *moon water (optional, see page 18), spring water, a kettle, your favourite tea, a cup and a spoon.*

If you have moon water, pour a small amount into your kettle, along with the spring water, then boil it. Add your teabag or leaves to a cup and pour in the water, letting it brew as usual. As you stir the tea, move your spoon clockwise to attract and manifest what you desire, or anticlockwise to banish negativity or unwanted influences.

As you sip your tea, focus on the intention you are sending out into the universe. Notice the energy flowing from you into the tea and then out into your life.

Quick abundance ritual

When finances feel tight, this speedy ritual can help invite abundance and attract unexpected opportunities.

YOU WILL NEED *1 teaspoon salt and 1 teaspoon ground cinnamon.*

Hold the salt in one hand and the cinnamon in the other. Rub your hands together as you visualize money coming your way. Do this for three minutes, then wash your hands. Money will come in unexpected ways.

★ Goals rebirth spell

Just as spring awakens the earth from its winter slumber, this spell helps awaken your intentions and ambitions. For best results, cast on a Monday, or during a new-moon phase.

YOU WILL NEED *yellow paper, a pen and scissors.*

Think about what you want for the next 6 to 12 months. It's very important that you visualize exactly how you will feel when you get what it is you want. What will your emotions be? Try to replicate the feelings as if your wishes have already come true.

Draw a large egg shape on the yellow paper, then write your wishes inside the egg shape. You can break down long-term goals into more manageable steps. For example, if you want to get a college degree in four years' time, write down that you have been accepted on the course.

When you've finished writing, cut around the egg shape, then roll it into a scroll. Find an area where you can bury the egg – a plant pot or in the earth in your garden. Bury the egg scroll. As the paper decomposes, your desires will slowly manifest.

Spring vitality tonic

This restorative tonic is perfect for lifting your spirits and boosting your energy. Traditionally made with elderberries, it can also be adapted with any seasonal berries you have on hand.

YOU WILL NEED *900g (2lb) seasonal berries, a heatproof pot with a lid, an orange (cut in half), 5 or 6 cloves, 100ml (3½fl oz) water, 450g (1lb) brown sugar, an oven, a wooden spoon, a sieve, a jug, a funnel and a glass bottle with a lid.*

Wash your berries, then place them in the heatproof pot. Add the orange, cloves, water and brown sugar. Cover the pot with a lid and place in a warm oven for 30 minutes to soften the fruit. Remove from the oven and leave to cool for 5 minutes, then stir, mashing the fruit with the wooden spoon. Strain the contents into the jug and allow the syrup to cool to room temperature.

Using a funnel, pour the contents of the jug into the glass bottle. Whenever you need a little pick-me-up, take 1 teaspoon of your witches' tonic. Your tonic will last for a month if kept refrigerated.

Crystal sun jar

Crystals are powerful magical tools, but they become even more potent when charged by the powers of the celestial bodies. While many know that moonlight can energize crystals, it is less commonly known that sunlight is equally powerful. This spell guides you to create a personalized crystal jar, infusing your crystals with solar power to amplify your magic.

YOU WILL NEED ***a selection of small crystals, a clear jar with a lid, a white tealight candle and matches.***

Crystals are very personal items, so always choose those that you feel drawn to. Before placing them in the jar, hold each crystal in your hands for a few minutes. You will notice that the crystal begins to feel warm. This means that it is now holding your energy.

Carefully place each crystal into the jar. Light your candle and place it in front of the jar, then allow it to safely burn away. Place the crystal jar somewhere you can see it every day. Whenever you need a crystal for a spell, pick one out of your jar which is already energized.

CRYSTAL CORRESPONDENCES
Amethyst – to relieve anxiety
Hematite – for serenity
Tiger's eye – for energy-cleansing
Quartz (clear, white and pink) – for love and positivity
Blue lace agate – for communication
Turquoise – for protection

Courage of the season spell

Anxiety can make it difficult to find your voice and stand tall. This courage spell uses Tarot and the goddess Bia to awaken your inner strength, giving you the confidence to act and speak with clarity. For best results, cast during a waxing-moon phase.

YOU WILL NEED *a Strength Tarot card (or a printout of one), an amethyst crystal, a purple iris (or another purple flower) and salt.*

Find a space to display your items where they won't be disturbed for a few days – your altar would be ideal. Take the Strength card and place it on a flat surface, then place the amethyst on top of it. Place the iris (or purple flower) on top of the crystal. Draw a circle of salt around the card. Say the following words out loud:

'I call upon Bia, the goddess of might, to help me in my need of courage right now. I know that you will be by my side with good intentions, and that you will be with me in my hour of need. Thank you, so mote it be.'

Leave the items in place for seven days. When you need courage, carry the amethyst, Strength card and flower with you.

Floral fortune spell

This spell channels the power of the spring goddess Eostre and the seasonal flora to bring good fortune into your space. Cast it as soon as fresh spring flowers are available.

YOU WILL NEED 6 *daffodils, tulips or other long-stemmed spring flowers, scissors, 6 silver pins, a vase and water.*

Lay your flowers out on a table and cut a small piece from the bottom of each stem. Take a pin and push it horizontally through the stem of one flower. As you do so, say the following words:

'Eostre, goddess of spring, I give you silver as an offering, in return for an abundance of good luck. I give you these flowers by way of thanks for your help and protection. So mote it be.'

Repeat this with each flower. Fill your vase two-thirds full with water and place the flowers one at a time into the vase. Place the vase somewhere you will see it every day. Every time you pass by, give thanks to Mother Nature for providing you with these beautiful flowers.

Your luck should increase within days. As the flowers fade, repeat the spell with a fresh bunch for consistent good luck.

Find your familiar

Spring is the time of new baby animals everywhere. Many witches believe that animals carry wisdom from the natural world and act as extensions of our spirits. Some are lifelong companions, known as familiars, while others walk beside us only during certain seasons of our journey. To discover your familiar, all you need to do is ask the universe and look for the signs.

YOU WILL NEED *a white candle and matches.*

Find a quiet, comfortable place and sit with your legs crossed. Light the candle and quiet your mind. Take a deep breath in and hold it for three counts, then exhale for the count of four. Fix your gaze on the flame of the candle. Out loud, say:

'I call upon the animal world to bring forth my spirit and guardian to me now. Please show yourself to me so that I may communicate with you from here on.'

Close your eyes and steady your breathing. An image may come into your mind of an animal, and this is a sign of who your animal spirit is. Don't worry if you don't see anything right away.

Over the following days, pay attention. You may come across the same animal repeatedly in pictures, dreams, books and conversations, or you may even encounter it in the wild. When it shows up more than once, take it as your sign. Your familiar is reaching out, ready to share its lessons and walk with you. You may already have a clue: perhaps an animal you adored as a child, or one you've always felt a fascination for but never questioned.

Guiding light blessing

When you feel at a crossroads in life, the right path can seem unclear. This spring blessing calls upon Hecate, the goddess of guidance and crossroads, to help illuminate your way. For best results, cast this spell on a quiet spring evening.

YOU WILL NEED *dried rosemary, dried thyme, dried sage, dried lavender, a small pouch, a black pen, a stone or pebble and a crossroads.*

Combine the dried herbs and place in the pouch. With your black pen, write a question mark on the stone or pebble. Next, find an area near your home where the roads or paths cross. Stand safely at the centre of the crossroads and place the stone in front of your feet. Begin to spin around in a clockwise direction and, as you do so, shake the herbs out of the pouch and say the following words:

'I call Hecate to come forth and guide me in the right direction. I walk in your shadow. I walk in your light. Come to me and make my decisions right tonight.'

Close your eyes and visualize the goddess Hecate rising up to help you in your quest. Leave the stone or pebble where it is and walk away without looking back. During your sleep that night, you should be given the answers to your questions.

Sanctuary discovery spell

This spell helps you find a spiritual place where you can recharge, reflect and connect with the natural energy of spring.

YOU WILL NEED *a couple of your favourite crystals.*

Go for a walk around your local area. Keep exploring until you find somewhere that connects with you. Even if you live in the city, you will find secret hideaways. Your spiritual place should be somewhere that is quiet and undisturbed by passers-by, where you feel you can sit in peace and quiet. Once you've found your spot, place your crystals there so that they absorb the natural energy. Sit for a few minutes and say:

***'I've found my spiritual place in time,
a place where I can relax and free my mind, of daily clutter and strife,
I thank you, Mother Nature, for being in my life.'***

Sit for as long as you wish in your spiritual place and feel nature's energy permeate your soul. Leave your crystals there overnight, so that they too absorb the magical energy. When you return, you can take your crystals home with you to use in future spells.

Try to get away to your spiritual place as often as you can to recharge.

Beltane fire blessing

Beltane, traditionally held on 1 May, is the fire festival that celebrates the transition of spring into summer. Fire represents both purification and passion, and this spell uses a miniature bonfire to set the stage for a joyful summer ahead. Perform this spell outside on the evening of 1 May, or as close to this date as possible.

YOU WILL NEED *a flower crown (see page 76 to make your own), a deep metal tray, fireproof dish or heat-safe cauldron, a handful of hay or straw, foraged twigs (roughly 25cm/10in long), matches and a bucket of water or sand for safety.*

Wearing your flower crown, head outside and place the tray, dish or cauldron securely on level ground. Add the hay or straw to the centre, then arrange the twigs around it in a small cone shape, like a miniature bonfire. Light the hay carefully, allowing the twigs to catch. Watch the flames rise, staying mindful of the fire. As it burns, give thanks by saying:

'Green Man, Lady May, protect us all on this fine day.
May blessings come, may blessings stay,
I give thanks to you for this wonderful day!'

As the fire begins to naturally die down, jump over it three times (being careful not to catch your clothing in the flames) to seal in the blessing. For safety, you can circle the bonfire three times instead or, once the flames have burned down, you may carefully step over the cooled ashes.

When you are finished, ensure the fire is fully extinguished using water or sand.

Beltane candle spell

Beltane is the celebration of fire, passion and revival, and this candle spell will help you align with these energies. For best results, perform this on Beltane evening.

YOU WILL NEED *a red candle, a white candle, a silver pin, fresh spring flowers, green ribbon, a few rose quartz crystals and matches.*

Carefully carve your first name into both candles using the pin. This personalizes the spell and ties the energies directly to you. Set the candles in their holders, then arrange the flowers, ribbon and rose quartz crystals around them to create a spring altar. Light both candles and say:

'I invite Brigid, Freyja and Eostre to gather with me in celebration of this Sabbat. May you bring joy, growth and renewal as I celebrate life. So mote it be.'

Spend a few minutes meditating on the candle flames, feeling the warmth of Beltane's fire filling you with vitality and fresh energy. Allow the candles to burn down safely. When finished, carry the rose quartz and green ribbon with you as talismans of Beltane's blessings. The flowers can be composted to return them to the earth as an offering of gratitude.

♥ May Day bonding ritual

Beltane, or May Day, is a time when communities gather to honour life's abundance. This ritual weaves together the threads of friendship, family and love, strengthening ties and bonds. Perform this ritual on Beltane to celebrate life with family and friends.

YOU WILL NEED *a picnic and drinks (to honour Beltane's spirit of feasting), a coloured ribbon for each participant (see list for colour symbolism), a blanket or rug and a large rose quartz crystal.*

If the weather permits, perform this ritual outdoors in the spring air; otherwise, it may be carried out indoors. Lay out the blanket and prepare the food and drink to share.

Sit together in a circle and ask each participant to choose a coloured ribbon. Tie all the ribbons together at one end, and place the rose quartz on top of the tied ends in the middle of the circle to charge the ribbons with loving energy and keep them steady. Each person should hold the non-tied end of their ribbon.

Nominate one person to begin. Holding their ribbon, they share aloud what they are most looking forward to in the coming season. They then pass their ribbon to the person on their right. The next person holds both ribbons (theirs and the one they have just received) and adds their own intention. This continues around the circle until everyone has spoken.

The final person gathers all the ribbons together and plaits them into a braid, symbolizing the weaving of everyone's hopes, joys and energies into one. Once finished, tie a knot at the end and wind the braid around the rose quartz.

Enjoy your feast together, celebrating your connections and the season of Beltane. Afterwards, keep the braided ribbons and rose quartz in the host's home as a sign of love, unity and shared blessings.

COLOUR CORRESPONDENCES
White – *peace, serenity, spirituality, mediumship*
Red – *energy, health, courage, passion, determination*
Pink – *love, romance, affection, harmony*
Yellow – *creativity, joy, fun, play*
Green – *abundance, prosperity, fertility, growth*
Blue – *inspiration, protection, ambition*
Purple – *wealth, psychic ability*
Silver – *clairvoyance, intuition*
Orange – *career, justice*
Gold – *money, happiness, contentment*
Black – *banishing, protecting, shielding*

Spring herb bundle

Around Beltane, the earth is alive with herbs and flowers bursting into bloom, making it the perfect time to craft a bundle to refresh your home, clear away stagnant winter energy and invite joy.

YOU WILL NEED *a collection of long-stemmed spring herbs or flowers, natural twine and matches.*

Gather your herbs and flowers and stack different stems on top of one another until you've created a log of foliage Starting at the base of the bundle, wind your twine tightly around the stems to secure them. Continue wrapping the string up the length of the bundle, pulling firmly to hold it in place. Leave a tail of string at the end.

Hang your bundle upside down in a warm, dry spot for several days.

Once fully dry, trim the string tail. Your bundle is now ready to use. Light the end, let it smoulder gently, and carry the bundle through your home to cleanse and fill your space with the fresh, renewing energy of spring. Remember: after burning your herb bundle, always collect the spent ash, as it will have absorbed the negative energy. Be sure to discard of it away from your home.

HERB CORRESPONDENCES
Lavender – peace
Rosemary – protection
Sage – cleansing
Mint – prosperity
Chamomile – calm
Rose – love
Thyme – courage

★ Beltane ancestor blessing

Alongside Samhain, Beltane is one of the two great times in the year when the veil between worlds grows thin, making it easier for us to connect with our ancestors and honour the wisdom they carry. For best results, perform this spell in the evening of Beltane.

YOU WILL NEED *a photo or keepsake of one of your ancestors, a cupcake, a birthday candle and matches.*

Place the photo or keepsake of your ancestor on a table and place the cupcake in front of it. Put the birthday candle into the centre of the cake and light it. Say the following words:

'(Name), I bless this day to remember you and all that you have done for me. I may not have known you, I may not have experienced your life, but I give thanks for you going before me and paving the way so that I may have a better life than you had. My thanks and love I send to you.'

Allow the candle to safely burn down and, if you like, eat the cake as you remember those who came before you and send them blessings. After doing this blessing, people often dream about their ancestors or relatives who have passed away. This is a sign that they have heard you and are still around you.

Beltane feast blessing

Beltane celebrates the arrival of warmer months and the energy of abundance. This feast ritual invites a vibrant summer ahead. Perform it on Beltane evening.

YOU WILL NEED *a selection of your favourite foods, table or picnic blanket, a fire pit and logs, incense sticks, dried mixed herbs and a cloth pouch.*

As the evenings grow lighter, it's a lovely time to celebrate outside with loved ones. Set out all your favourite foods on a table or picnic blanket near your fire pit. Set up the fire, placing some incense sticks in between the logs, and light the fire. Prior to eating, give thanks to the universe for all your blessings, then give everyone a handful of dried herbs. Ask them to put their herbs into the cloth bag.

When the bag is full, throw it into the fire as an offering to the gods and goddesses who are looking out for you.

Enjoy your outdoor feast! Beltane is also a day of dancing, so try to incorporate this into your evening too.

★ Morning dew Beltane wish

According to folklore, the morning dew on 1 May carries special manifesting powers. Washing your face in this dew while making a wish can help bring your desires to life.

YOU WILL NEED *a patch of dew-covered grass.*

Think about what it is you desire the night before Beltane, then get up early before the sun rises. Find a nice, clean grassy area and rub your hands over the grass, giving thanks to Mother Nature. Rub the dew all over your face and let it air-dry. Magical things will begin to happen in your life!

♥ Daisy chain love spell

This spell uses the natural energy of spring flora to attract a loving, harmonious relationship. For best results, cast on a Friday.

YOU WILL NEED *2 pink candles, matches, 10 daisies with stalks (or another seasonal weed flower), a rose quartz crystal and a pink envelope.*

Light the two pink candles and sit in front of them as you make a daisy chain by piercing the stalk of one flower and threading the next flower into the hole. Repeat this process until you have a string of ten daisies in a row, then push the last daisy into a hole in the first stalk to create a ring of flowers.

Carefully place your daisy chain over the pink candles and place the quartz crystal in front of the candle. Say the following words:

***'From one to ten, the spell is cast,
bring to me a love that will last.
A love of equal measure,
a love that I will treasure.
From ten to one, the spell is done.
Freyja will help me, so mote it be.'***

Just before the candles have safely burned away, place the daisy chain in the envelope and seal it with warm wax from the candles. Place the crystal on top of the envelope and leave it in a safe place for the next 28 days.

♥ Spring love potion

With the arrival of spring, the world feels full of romantic possibility. This love potion will lift your spirits, make you feel irresistible and attract admirers. For best results, cast on a Friday.

YOU WILL NEED *an empty bottle, a bottle of bubble bath, spring water, rose essential oil, lavender essential oil, sandalwood essential oil, tea tree essential oil, lemon essential oil, rose petals and a bathtub.*

Half-fill the empty bottle with bubble bath. Add the spring water until it's almost two-thirds full and give it a little shake (with the lid on!). Add three drops of each of the essential oils, followed by a few rose petals. Place the lid on again and turn the bottle upside down several times so that all the oils mix together.

Run yourself a bath and pour a couple of capfuls of your love potion into the water – if you don't have a bathtub, you can use the potion in the shower by washing yourself with it. As you enter the water, say the following words:

'I'm ready to step into spring with new loves and admirers. I ask that you send only those pure in heart and soul. So mote it be.'

Relax in the tub as you visualize a wonderful love life heading your way. Dry yourself off and keep the rest of the love potion for future use. It will keep for at least three months.

Spring success spell

Spring is a season of growth and fresh opportunities, making it an ideal time to call success into your life. Use this spell to invite prosperity, confidence and achievement. For best results, cast on a Thursday.

YOU WILL NEED *paper, a green pen, a green tealight candle and matches.*

Sit for a while and decide what success means to you at the moment. Really think about what it is you need in order to feel successful. Write it down on the piece of paper using your green pen, in just one sentence.

Now you need to fold the paper into a paper boat – if you don't know how to do this, you can find instructions online. Take your paper boat to a river or canal. Light your tealight candle and place it near the river. Drop your paper boat into the water and watch it sail away into the universe. Wait until the tealight has safely burned away, then take the empty holder back to your home and dispose of it. Success is now on its way.

Prosperous spring candle spell

Spring is the perfect time to invite prosperity into your life. This candle spell is designed to attract financial blessings and opportunities. For best results, cast it on a Friday, or during a full-moon phase.

YOU WILL NEED *2 bank notes, a green candle, a gold candle, 2 dried bay leaves and matches.*

Set up a space where your spell won't be disturbed for 48 hours. Lay the bank notes on a flat surface and place the green candle in a candle holder on top of one and the gold candle in a candle holder on top of the other. Take one dried bay leaf and tuck it into the space between the candle and candle holder of the green candle. Repeat with the gold candle.

Light the green candle first, followed by the gold candle. Repeat the following three times:

'Money and prosperity come to me.
Money grows and money flows.
Candles burn and see me earn.
Worries fade from this day.
Blessed Be, to me.'

As the candles burn down, the bay leaves will catch light, and they might spit and crackle a little. Once this happens, the spell is complete, and you can blow out the candles. Leave the bank notes and spell in place for 48 hours, then place the bank notes back into your purse and clear away the rest of the spell.

Spring goddess brew

Spring is a season of ripening fresh fruit, whether gathered from gardens, markets or your local shop. This spell fills your home with the sweet scent of the season, while inviting the blessing and protection of spring goddesses (see page 61). For best results, cast during a new-moon phase.

YOU WILL NEED *a selection of spring fruits (such as rhubarb, strawberries, gooseberries or cherries), a cinnamon stick, a saucepan, water, fruit peelings and a toothpick.*

Combine the fruits and the cinnamon stick in your saucepan, then top up with water. Place over a low heat – just enough to heat the mixture.

If you want to make a wish to the goddesses, use the toothpick to etch the wish on to some fruit peelings and add them to the pot. Allow the mixture to simmer, stirring occasionally, all day long. As the fruits break down, your home will be filled with a natural magical fragrance that will encourage the goddesses in.

For an extra layer of protection, drink a cup of the fruit punch once cooled, or freeze portions for future spells.

Job change spell

Spring is the season of new beginnings, meaning now is the ideal time to manifest a new job or even a complete career change. For best results, cast outside or in a well-ventilated space on a Monday or during a new-moon phase.

YOU WILL NEED *3 mint leaves, a pen, 3 bay leaves, paper, matches and a fireproof dish or cauldron.*

Place the mint leaves on a flat surface and, on each leaf, write one specific thing that you love to do and would still do even if you weren't paid to do it. This could be something like playing with puppies all day long or meeting new people. Next, on each of the bay leaves, write an ideal job title – something you would love to do.

Place a mint leaf on top of each bay leaf, so that you have three little piles of leaves. Take your sheet of paper and write the following words:

'Show me my dream job and bring it to me.'

Put all the leaves in the centre of the paper and fold the paper into three so that all the leaves are inside it.

Set fire to the paper (with the leaves inside) and allow it to safely burn away in your dish or cauldron. Pay attention to signs and opportunities that suggest a new job or career manifesting in your life.

♥ New baby blessing

This gentle spell can help protect a little one from harm, keeping them safe and surrounded by positive energy. It can be cast at any time to bless and safeguard either a new baby or an older child in your life.

YOU WILL NEED *1 teaspoon dried lavender, 1 teaspoon dried rosemary, 1 teaspoon dried sage, a pinch of sugar, a pinch of salt, a bowl, a small teddy or other soft toy, scissors, a sewing needle, thread and blue ribbon.*

Combine the lavender, rosemary, sage, sugar and salt in a bowl and mix them together with the index finger of your dominant hand. Repeat the following words as you mix:

'I call upon the goddesses Brigid, Freyja and Eostre to protect this infant from harm for evermore. I call upon you to shield them from harm and hate. I call upon you to bring only good fortune their way, today and every day, for evermore. So be it now.'

Carefully unstitch the left side of the teddy or soft toy, close to where the heart would be. Pour your mixed ingredients into the toy, then stitch it back together. Stitch the ribbon to the top of the toy in a loop.

Hang the toy above the baby's crib (or child's bed) to protect from any harm.

♥ Wiccan bridal charm bag

Spring is a season of love and new ventures, making it a common time of year for weddings and romantic unions. This charm bag is a thoughtful gift for someone who is about to marry, and is designed to bring happiness to the couple. Perform this spell on the night before the wedding.

YOU WILL NEED *a handful of dried lavender, a handful of dried mint or mint leaves, a handful of ground allspice, a small red charm bag, 2 red rose petals, lavender essential oil, rose essential oil, 1 metre (3ft) pink ribbon and a safety pin.*

Combine the lavender, mint and allspice in the charm bag and shake them up. Add the rose petals and three drops each of lavender and rose oil. Say the following words:

'This magic mix will bring magic to the marriage. This magic mix will bring happiness, love and laughter for evermore. So mote it be.'

Tie the pouch together with the pink ribbon and, on the eve of the wedding day, give it to the bride or groom to place under their pillow. This will neutralize any worries about the following day.

On the morning of the wedding, instruct the bride or groom to pin the pouch to the inside of their wedding outfit to bless the marriage.

♥ Spring heart attraction spell

Spring is the perfect time to invite love into your life. For best results, cast outside or in a well-ventilated space on a Friday night, preferably at midnight.

YOU WILL NEED *pink paper, a red or pink pen, a pink tealight candle, rose petals, a rose quartz crystal and a fireproof dish or cauldron.*

On the pink paper, write down what you want out of a relationship, using the pink or red pen. Think about the kind of partner you want and how you want the relationship to look, and write it down.

Light your candle and scatter the rose petals in a circle around it. Hold the rose quartz in your hand and say:

'I hereby declare my request for new love to enter my life. They will fulfil all my desires in a lover, and I will not settle for less than I deserve. So mote it be.'

Light the pink paper with the flame from the candle and drop it into the fireproof dish or cauldron, then blow out the candle. Let the paper safely burn away, then wait for the ashes to cool. When the ashes are cool, place the rose petals and rose quartz on top of them, then place the dish or cauldron under your bed for the next 48 hours. Dispose of the ashes and petals, and keep the crystal under your pillow until your perfect person shows up.

Money manifestation charm

Spring is a time of growth and abundance, making it a good time for prosperity spells. This simple spell helps invite wealth into your life. For best results, cast on a Friday before midnight.

YOU WILL NEED *a small glass, 3 silver coins, a pinch of ground cinnamon, 3 mint leaves, rice, a green candle and matches.*

Wash and dry the glass to get rid of any negative energy. Place the silver coins into the bottom of the glass, followed by a pinch of cinnamon and the mint leaves. Fill the glass with rice, then push the green candle about 2.5cm (1in) into the rice. Light the candle and say the following words:

'I ask the universe to provide me with more than enough now. I pray to Brigid to bring forth new wealth energy to me. So mote it be.'

Allow the candle to burn away, then dispose of the ingredients – apart from the silver coins. Keep these in a safe place as a lucky charm. More money should come your way very soon.

Pendulum divination spell

Pendulums are used to gain insight, guidance and clarity. While you can buy one, crafting your own adds personal energy and intention to your practice. For best results, cast this spell during a full-moon phase.

YOU WILL NEED *a chain or leather cord, a pendulum, pendant or hanging crystal, your favourite essential oil, a white tealight candle, matches, a circle of card and a pen.*

Begin by putting together your magical pendulum. Your chain or leather cord should be long enough to hang by about 25cm (10in), and the pendulum needs to be heavy enough that it just hangs when the chain or cord is held between your finger and thumb and doesn't sway at the slightest breeze.

Sprinkle a few drops of essential oil on the pendulum, then the candle. Light your candle and hold your pendulum 10cm (4in) above the flame, so that the heat purifies it but doesn't burn it. Swing your pendulum above the flame and ask the universe to bless and purify it with fire for a minute or two.

Next, take your circle of card and divide it into three by drawing three equal lines so that it looks like a pie. In one section write the word 'YES', in the next write the word 'NO', and in the third draw a question mark.

Hold the pendulum in your hands and take three deep breaths. Lean your elbow on the table and hang the pendulum over the sheet of paper. Test the pendulum by asking it a question that you already know the answer to, such as 'Is a ball round?' The pendulum should begin to swing to the 'YES'. This might take a little time, so be patient.

Now you can ask your spirit guides any yes/no question you wish. Just hold the pendulum cord or chain between your finger and thumb over the card circle, and its movement will provide you with an answer. If it can't give you an answer right now, it will point to the question mark.

★ Spring wish paper

This spell allows you to make your own magical paper infused with the energy of spring, ready to carry your wishes into the universe. For best results, cast this spell on a sunny spring morning.

YOU WILL NEED *a bowl, warm water (moon water is great if you have it, see page 18), 5 paper towels, a rolling pin (optional), a towel, small spring flowers of your choice and a pen.*

Fill a bowl with warm water and add the paper towels. Swish them around so that they soak up the water and begin to dissolve into a mush. Scoop the mush out of the water and form it into a ball. Squeeze out all the excess water, then use your hands to massage the wet paper ball into a thin rectangle – you might want to use a rolling pin. Once you have formed your rectangle, place it on a towel.

Pick the petals from your spring flowers and sprinkle them all over the wet paper rectangle, then leave it to dry on a sunny windowsill.

When it's completely dry, you will have a sheet of floral paper. Take your pen and write down one wish. Keep your wish paper somewhere safe until your wish is granted.

♥ Spring gathering blessing

Spring is the perfect season for celebration, connection and community. This spell is all about sharing blessings and good fortune, so it is ideal for casting prior to a party or gathering. For best results, perform it on a weekend.

YOU WILL NEED *paper, a pen, ingredients for your favourite cookie recipe, a mixing bowl, a wooden spoon, a baking tray, baking paper and an oven.*

Prior to making your cookies, ask your friends or family to name one thing they wish for. Write their answers down on a piece of paper so you remember them.

Make your favourite cookie batter. When you're ready to stir the mixture, whisper the first person's wish into the bowl, then stir the mixture three times in a clockwise direction. Repeat this whispering and stirring until you have named all the wishes and the batter is well mixed.

Line a baking tray with baking paper. As you spoon dollops of the cookie dough on to the baking paper, say the following words:

'As I've mixed, this is my wish:
may you grant all desires with the heat of fire.
So mote it be.'

Place the cookies in the oven. As they bake, visualize all those wishes being granted. When the cookies have cooled, share them with your friends, family or coven.

Basil wealth ritual

Basil has long been known in folklore as a powerful attractor of wealth and prosperity. This simple ritual helps draw abundance into your life. For best results, cast this spell on a Friday.

YOU WILL NEED *4 potted basil plants.*

Place one potted plant in each corner of your home downstairs. This will attract wealth to you. If you don't have plants, you can just use basil leaves and replace them monthly.

The power of three

Across cultures, the number three has held extraordinary significance, from the Three Fates of Greek mythology to the Christian Trinity, the Three Wise Men and even the Wiccan Threefold Law. It is believed to magnify intention and energy in all things, and you can easily incorporate the power of three into your home.

YOU WILL NEED *paper, scissors, a pen and sticky tape.*

Use the scissors to cut the paper into several small pieces. On each piece, draw a triangle to represent the power of three. Use the tape to stick these triangles on the walls in different rooms of your home to attract good health, wealth and positive energy into your living space.

Abundance chant

Spring is a great time for inviting prosperity into your life. Use this chant to align yourself with the energy of abundance and set the tone for a financially flourishing season.

YOU WILL NEED *a crossroads.*

Find an area near your home where the roads or paths cross. Stand safely at the centre, close your eyes and say the following words:

'With all these roads, a beautiful sight,
bring prosperity into my sight.
In you I trust, to you I pray,
bring wealth back to me today.'

Walk away, confident that the universe will grant your wish.

SUMMER

In the Wiccan calendar, summer is the season of abundance. The sun is at its strongest, and nature overflows with life. Crops ripen, flowers bloom and the warmth of the season draws us outdoors to celebrate the earth's riches. This is when the efforts of spring come to fruition, and we are invited to enjoy the rewards of growth and manifestation. Across most of Europe, summer stretches from June through August. Even in different climates the themes of summer remain the same: vitality, joy, fulfilment and gratitude.

Summer festivals & celebrations

Litha *(Midsummer/Summer Solstice)*

Litha falls between 19 and 23 June, depending on where you are in the world. It marks the longest day of the year when the sun reaches the highest point in the sky. The word 'solstice' comes from the Latin *solstitum*, which means 'the sun stood still'. From this day onward, the hours of daylight gradually shorten, reminding us of the cyclical balance of light and dark.

In the Celtic and Druidic traditions, Litha was a celebration of fire and fertility. Today, many Pagans and Wiccans still celebrate Litha by gathering at sacred sites such as Stonehenge or Glastonbury to watch the sunrise, honouring the life-giving energy of the sun and giving thanks for a bountiful harvest. Rituals include lighting bonfires, enjoying picnics and barbecues, dancing and decorating homes with summer flowers.

This is a powerful Sabbat for spells of gratitude, abundance and protection. It is also a time to honour how far we've come and set intentions for the months ahead.

Lughnasadh *(Lammas)*

Lughnasadh, celebrated on 1 or 2 August, marks the first harvest of the year and the midway point between summer and autumn. The name comes from the Celtic sun god Lugh, who was believed to bless the crops. When the harvest was gathered, his life cycle was complete.

Traditionally, this was a time of feasting, games and gatherings. In Scotland, Lughnasadh often stretched into an eleven-day festival of food, drink and merriment. In times gone by, this period was also popular for what were known as trial weddings. A couple would have a mock wedding and live together for a year and a day. If they decided they were not suited, they could part ways without consequence. If their union was successful, they would tie coloured ribbons into a knot and marry for real the following year. This gave rise to the expression 'tie the knot'.

Lughnasadh is a time for rituals of prosperity, contracts, handfastings and business ventures, honouring the balance between reaping rewards and planning for the future.

Summer goddesses

Sol

Sol is the ancient Norse goddess of the sun, and her job is to nourish the earth and humankind. We worship Sol during Midsummer with bonfires. Sol brings light to any situation and is often called upon when we feel lost in the dark.

Demeter

Demeter is the ancient Greek goddess of the harvest and represents motherhood and fertility. She also governs law and justice, and was the sister of the gods Zeus, Hera, Hades, Poseidon and Hestia, so she is especially powerful. You should call upon Demeter for help with moving forwards in life.

Isis

Isis is a powerful Egyptian goddess who is known for her maternal magic. She protects against illness and is seen as the nurturing mother. Isis is fiercely protective of all who worship her, so she's an ideal goddess to call upon if you are seeking protection.

Summer tips & recommendations

Ingredient access

Summer provides an abundance of fresh herbs and flowers, perfect for spellwork and kitchen witchery. This is the best time to gather lavender, rosemary, sage, parsley, thyme, chamomile, sunflowers, marigolds and rose petals. Preserve what you collect for use in the autumn and winter months. It is best to use the power of the sun, rather than artificial heat, to dry herbs and seeds, as this gives them more natural power.

Observing nature

Spend time outdoors to connect with the rhythm of the season. Midsummer walks, swims in rivers or lakes and barefoot rituals in the grass are all ways to honour the season's energy.

Crafting tools

This is an ideal time to create flower crowns, herb bundles, corn dollies and sun wheels. Collect seeds for future planting and press summer blooms to use in spell jars, journals or charms.

Best spell types for summer

Summer is particularly potent for spells of abundance, release, joy, community, strength and protection. Rituals of gratitude and future-forward spells are especially powerful during this time.

SUMMER SPELLS

Solstice step forward spell

The Summer Solstice marks the longest day of the year, when the sun is at its peak and energy is ripe for change. This is the perfect time to step into the season with intention. Cinnamon is a powerful spice for summoning this fresh summer feeling of prosperity and success.

YOU WILL NEED *a pinch of ground cinnamon.*

Before putting on your socks and shoes, sprinkle a small amount of dried cinnamon into the palms of your hands and rub it on to the soles of your feet. Then put your socks and shoes on as normal. Let the spice guide you to release the old and welcome the new, carrying the energy of the Solstice with you as you step into summer.

Summer health spell

The summer season may bring sunshine, but it also brings seasonal sniffles and hay fever. This magical herbal cuppa will help restore your vitality, keeping you healthy when pollen is rife.

YOU WILL NEED *a jug, boiling water, a pinch of ground ginger, a cinnamon stick, 4 cloves, 1 teaspoon honey, a spoon, a strainer and a cup or mug.*

Pour the water into a jug, then add the ginger, cinnamon stick, cloves and honey. Stir and allow to steep for a few minutes, then strain the liquid into a mug and drink. You can make this magic tea anytime you need a pick-me-up.

Protective arrow spell

This spell uses a protective Wiccan symbol to safeguard against harmful energies.

YOU WILL NEED *a black non-permanent pen.*

On your left palm, draw an arrow pointing upwards, then draw a cross through the long part of the arrow (see reference image on right).

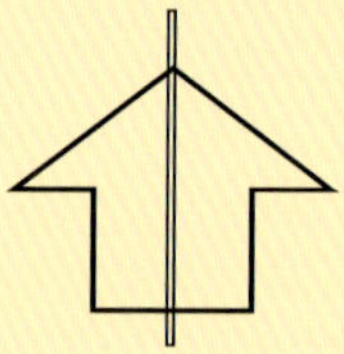

Summer herb bundle

Herbs are full of the sun's power. Crafting a fresh bundle at the start of summer draws on the season's vibrancy, filling your home with warmth and protection.

YOU WILL NEED *dried lavender sprigs, dried sage sprigs, dried thyme sprigs, dried lemon balm sprigs, dried mint sprigs, natural twine, small flowers and matches.*

Make sure your herbs are fully dried, as this means they will burn longer. Gather them into a bundle and tie tightly together with the twine. Make sure you apply a bit of pressure so that the herbs are tightly packed together. When you're happy with your bundle, poke a few flowers into it.

To use the summer herb bundle, light the end with a match. Let it smoulder gently, and carry the bundle through your home, wafting the smoke to cleanse your space and fill it with the vibrant energies of summer.

Remember: after burning a herb bundle, always collect the spent ash, as it will have absorbed the negative energy. Be sure to discard of it away from your home.

Summer transformation spell

The start of summer brings longer days, brighter skies and the perfect chance to leave behind what no longer serves you. To banish any stale energy, cast this spell on a Sunday evening.

YOU WILL NEED *matches, a black tealight candle, an orange tealight candle, a yellow tealight candle, 3 lemon incense cones, a fireproof dish or cauldron and a sprig of rosemary.*

Sit and meditate on what it is you want to change about yourself. Who do you want to be next? You have this incredible power within you to change who you are. Light the black tealight candle and think about banishing the parts you don't like about yourself or your life. Allow this candle to safely burn away before moving on.

Now you have banished what you don't want to be, light the orange and yellow candles. Place the incense cones in your dish or cauldron, then light them. Now light the sprig of rosemary and drop this into the dish or cauldron too.

Breathe in the fragrance, visualizing yourself being reinvented and invigorated with magical powers to do and be anything you want.

Allow the candles and cones to burn safely away, then begin planning the changes you wish to make in your life. Your magical intention will bring them forth.

Litha assertiveness spell

The Summer Solstice, or Litha, is the time of the year when the sun is at its peak, bringing maximum energy. This is the perfect moment to harness that bold solar power to reinforce your personal boundaries. For best results, cast anytime during Litha.

YOU WILL NEED *a black tealight candle, matches, paper, a black pen, a sprig of sage, 1 teaspoon black salt, 1 teaspoon chilli flakes, a small red chilli and a glass jar with a lid.*

Light your candle, then sit and write down all the things you want to say no to but haven't felt able to. No one is going to see this, so write whatever comes to mind. This could be anything from constant requests from your boss to work overtime, or a friend asking you for money.

Place the sage, black salt, chilli flakes and whole chilli into the jar, followed by the piece of paper. Blow gently into the jar to set your intentions, then place the lid on. Drip some wax from your candle around the lid to seal it. Shake the jar and say the following words:

'I call on the goddess Isis to protect me when I say, no is a full sentence. No means no. No longer will I justify why I say no. So mote it be.'

Blow out the candle and dispose of it. Every time you are tempted to say yes to something you don't want to do, shake the jar for a minute to reset yourself.

Summer broom blessing

This spell blesses your broom, turning it into a personal talisman for summer magic. For best results, cast it during a full-moon phase.

YOU WILL NEED *a broom (see page 24 if you want to make one), sandalwood essential oil, different-coloured ribbons, a glue gun and glue, dried summer flowers, biodegradable glitter and any personal jewellery items you wish to add (optional).*

Your broom doesn't have to be a witches' broom; any broom will do, so long as it has a long stick. First, sprinkle several drops of sandalwood oil on to the broom handle and allow it to soak into the wood.

Now decorate! Tie the coloured ribbons around the handle and secure in place with some hot glue, then add your dried flowers and glitter. If you have some old jewellery that you'd like to include, attach this to your broomstick to make it more personal to you.

When you've finished, bless the broom by saying the following words:

***'I bless you broom, I make you mine,
to help me when needed, my true divine.'***

Keep your broom near the entrance of your home, with the bristles facing upwards if you want to attract people and downwards if you wish to be left alone.

Remember, never take an old broom to a new home. If you move house, create a new broom and leave the old one behind.

Summer energy boost spell

When you feel worn down by work, obligations or draining connections, the summer sun can help replenish your spirit. When you want to recharge your inner reserves, cast this spell on a bright day.

YOU WILL NEED *an open space and a warm, sunny day.*

Find a quiet area, preferably somewhere where you can feel the natural ground beneath your feet, such as a beach, a forest or a grassy lawn. Take off your shoes and socks and feel the earth beneath you.

Reach your arms above your head in the direction of the sun, as if performing a sun salutation. Close your eyes and take a deep breath as you feel the sun's rays hit you. Say the following words, to yourself or out loud:

'Demeter, by your summer power, I call my energy back to me from every person, place or entity that has stolen or borrowed it. No longer will I give away my energy freely. Every connection and attachment will use their own power and will not be allowed to drain mine without my consent. I now call my power back to me.'

Remain standing for as long as you wish until you feel your energy and power returning. You will soon notice that people who drain you no longer have access to your energy.

Fire 'lantern' wish spell

Witches use the fire element to carry intentions upwards, releasing wishes into the universe with the rising heat and light. This adapted version of the traditional fire lantern spell allows you to make a wish while honouring the flame in an environmentally friendly way. For best results, cast at night-time on or around Litha when the sun is at its strongest.

YOU WILL NEED *a large paper bag, scissors, a pen, a tealight candle in a heatproof holder and matches.*

Begin by cutting shapes into both sides of the paper bag. Stars, suns and spirals are particularly powerful symbols of Litha, but follow your intuition. On the outside of the bag, write down the wish you want to send into the universe. Be clear but concise.

Open the paper bag fully and place it on a stable surface outdoors, away from strong winds or dry foliage. Place the tealight candle (in its holder) inside the bag and carefully light it. The cut-out shapes will glow, flickering like magical fireflies dancing in the night. As the flame burns, focus on your wish being lifted by the fire's energy and carried skyward with the light.

Stay with the bag until the candle has safely burned out. When it has, dispose of the bag responsibly.

Summer Solstice altar

The Summer Solstice or Litha is a time when the sun's energy is at its most radiant. Creating an altar on this day anchors the solar magic of the season into your home, giving you a dedicated space for joy, strength and spells of abundance.

YOU WILL NEED *a mirror, an orange candle, a yellow candle, summer flowers, dried orange slices, orange incense and matches.*

Set up your altar in an area where it won't be disturbed. First add the mirror to reflect the summer's energy into your life. Place the candles in front of the mirror and decorate the rest of the space with the flowers, orange slices and incense.

Light candles and incense and say the following to open your altar:

'I invite Demeter, Sol and Isis to my altar. A safe space to gather and bring joy, peace and love into the world. When we come together, we become powerful. So mote it be.'

Blow out the candles and allow the incense to burn down. Your new summer altar is now activated and ready to use as a place to perform your summer spells.

★ Summer Solstice moon wish spell

The Strawberry Moon marks the first full moon of summer and coincides with Litha. Use this spell to harness both lunar and solar energies and manifest your desires. For best results, cast in the evening during a full-moon phase.

YOU WILL NEED *a lemon, a knife, a bowl, a quill or large feather, paper and a pink quartz crystal.*

Cut the lemon in half and squeeze its juice into a bowl. Remove and set aside any pips. Sit outside when the moon is full and dip your quill or feather into the lemon juice. Take your paper and write down one wish you want granted. Allow the lemon juice to dry, then hold the paper up to the moon and say:

'Luna goddess, Luna fair,
this is my wish, I do declare.
I hand it to you to grant with your lunar ways, may you grant me my wish, within 28 days. So mote it be.'

Place the paper on the ground and then place the pink quartz on top of it. Leave the paper outside in a safe spot until the next full moon.

If you have some soil and a pot available, you can plant the lemon pips you saved. They won't grow into a lemon tree, but they will produce small lemon-scented leaves, which you can then use in future spells.

Midsummer harvest blessing

Litha, also known as Midsummer's Day, is the ideal time to gather herbs, flowers and berries for spells, teas, tonics and charms. For best results, perform in the morning of Midsummer's Day.

YOU WILL NEED *a basket or natural bag, scissors or secateurs and gloves.*

Go for a walk, appreciating everything that Mother Nature freely provides us. When you come to a naturally growing plant that you like, ask it if you may borrow some, then cut a small branch or a few leaves from the plant. Wildlife rely on our plants and flowers, so only take as much as you need. Depending on where you live, you'll find plenty of herbs, grasses, flowers and leaves.

Make sure that you research what you have picked. There are free apps available that can identity a particular plant and tell you whether it's poisonous or not, so you can make sure your harvest is safe.

When you return home, gather what you have foraged in bunches, then hang them upside down somewhere warm and leave them to dry out. Once dry, you can store your summer harvest for future spells.

Crystal-infused water spell

Like all the elements, water is a powerful conduit for energy. This spell transforms the simple act of drinking water into a ritual for drawing positive energy into your life. For best results, cast this spell in the evening.

YOU WILL NEED *a water bottle, drinking water, a white quartz crystal, an amethyst crystal, a rose quartz crystal and a mystical sticker.*

Wash your water bottle out to get rid of any negative energy from the day before. Refill your water bottle with drinking water. Place the bottle on a flat surface and arrange the three crystals around the water bottle so that they form a triangle shape. Place the lid back on the bottle and hold your hand over the bottle. As you do so, say the following words:

'Water is life, life is mine,
behold the magic intertwine.
My quest is for positive energy,
here we go, so mote it be.'

Finally, place your mystical sticker somewhere on your water bottle and leave it in place until the following morning.

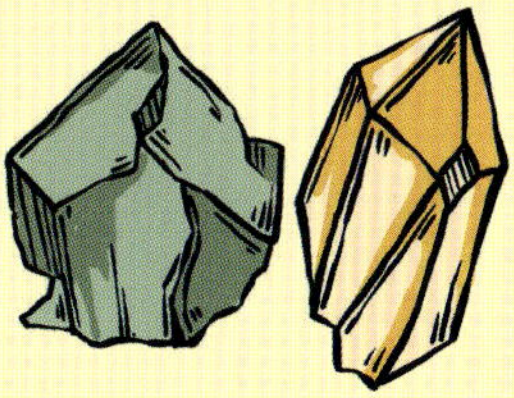

Solar water spell

The sun's light is just as powerful as the moon's, and creating solar water allows you to bottle that power, ready to use whenever you wish to enhance your summer spellwork. For best results, cast this spell on any sunny day.

YOU WILL NEED *a clear jar or bottle with lid, water, lemon, a peeler, a small clear quartz crystal and a piece of netting.*

Fill your jar or bottle with ordinary tap water. Peel the lemon and drop the peel into the water. Add a squeeze or two of lemon juice, then drop the quartz into the water too. Take the jar or bottle outside and place a piece of netting over the top to prevent bugs getting in. Place it in direct sunlight, somewhere where it won't get knocked over. Look up into the sky and say the following words:

'By the power of the goddess Sol, I ask that you purify this water and turn it into sun water. May you use your power of sunlight rays to transform. I thank you for your warmth and light in my life. So mote it be.'

Leave your water outside until dusk. It will now be energized with the power of the sun. Use it when you need solar-charged water for a spell. If you like, you can even drink it – just take out the crystal and lemon peel first.

★ Four flowers wish spell

Harness the gentle energy of summer blooms to bring your summer wishes to life. For best results, cast this spell in the morning on a sunny day.

YOU WILL NEED *4 flowerheads from different flowers.*

Find a quiet spot outside in the sunshine where you will be undisturbed. Take off your shoes and socks, then sit down on the grass, with your legs crossed and back straight. Take your four different flowerheads and place one in front of you, one to the left of you, one to the right of you and one behind you. Close your eyes and breathe in deeply for the count of four, then exhale for the count of four. This will ground you. Now think about what it is that you wish for in your life right now. Visualize it happening without much effort from yourself. Repeat the following words four times:

'By the power of one, my spell's begun.
By the power of two, I send to you.
By the power of three, I cast to thee.
By the power of four, grant my wish to me.'

If you don't feel comfortable saying this out loud, just say it in your head four times. The spell is now cast. Take the four flowerheads and put them in different locations, such as hedges or trees, to give them back to nature for wildlife to use.

Star anise protection spell

Star anise has been used in Chinese medicine for thousands of years, and in Wiccan practice, its star-shaped form is considered a powerful symbol of protection.

YOU WILL NEED *star anise.*

To safeguard your sacred space during rituals or spellwork, place a single star anise in each corner of your altar or workspace. As you place each star anise, visualize a protective light radiating from each corner, forming a safe and sacred circle around you. Its energy will help ward off negativity and unwanted influences.

If whole star anise is not available, you can also use ground star anise, as it carries the same protective properties. This can be sprinkled around your ritual area or added to your spell ingredients.

Solar eye protection spell

In ancient Egyptian magic, the Solar Eye of Ra was believed to offer divine protection, warding off negativity and danger. Working with this fiery symbol during the summer months calls upon the sun's strength to safeguard you.

YOU WILL NEED *4 large bay leaves and a pen.*

On each bay leaf, draw the solar eye as shown below:

Now place the bay leaves on top of each other in a pile. Hold them between the palms of your hands and repeat the following words:

'By the power of Ra, I call upon you to protect me. By the power of Ra, I call upon you to protect mine. By the power of Ra, I call upon you to protect my home. By the power of Ra, I call upon you to protect me from the unknown. By the power of Ra, I call upon you to protect all I love. By the power of Ra, I call to you above.'

Visualize the power of the sun's rays infusing the bay leaves with protective power. Your palms should begin to feel warm. Hold this visualization for ten minutes.

After you've done this, take your bay leaves outside and place one in each corner of your garden. If you don't have a garden, place one in each corner of your home. You will now be protected by Ra.

Summer confidence spell

Summer is the season of standing tall in your own power. This simple yet potent spell helps you draw on that energy whenever you need a boost of self-belief.

YOU WILL NEED *a notebook and a pen.*

On a blank page in your notebook, write one positive affirmation to yourself.

Tear the page out of your journal and leave it somewhere you will see it regularly, such as on your bedside table. It doesn't matter if you don't believe it at first; you will see the message every day, and it will begin to sink in.

Crystal garden sanctuary guide

This outdoor crystal arrangement amplifies the vibrant solar energy, turning your garden into a summer sanctuary.

YOU WILL NEED *a moss agate crystal, a green aventurine crystal, several tiger's eye crystals, 4 onyx crystals and a clear quartz crystal.*

Place the moss agate (also known as the 'gardener's stone') near plants to promote growth, healing and abundance. Place the green aventurine near new shoots or buds to stimulate new growth, vitality and luck in the garden. Place the tiger's eyes along the perimeter of your garden or window pots to act as a protective shield. Place the onyx in the corners or near vulnerable plants to repel negative energies and unwanted pests. Finally, place the quartz in the centre of your garden or window pots to amplify the energies of the other stones.

Sunstone Solstice spell

Harness the peak energy of Midsummer to focus on your dreams and intentions. This spell uses a sunstone to amplify your goals and bring clarity, helping you step confidently toward the future you desire. For best results, cast this spell on or around the Summer Solstice.

YOU WILL NEED *paper, a pen and a sunstone crystal.*

Write down who you wish to be in a year's time. Place the sunstone on top of the piece of paper in the sunshine and leave it until dusk. Afterwards, keep the piece of paper somewhere safe and carry the sunstone with you until your dream comes true.

Summer soulmate spell

With the blessing of Venus and the warmth of the summer sun, this spell calls love into your life, drawing a soulmate connection that reflects the joy and brightness of the season. For best results, cast it on a Friday – the day of love, beauty and attraction.

YOU WILL NEED *a saucepan, water, pink candle wax, red candle wax, 2 heatproof bowls, lavender essential oil, rose essential oil, a sprig of fresh lavender and matches.*

Half-fill the saucepan with water and bring a simmer. Place one heatproof bowl over the pan, then add the pink candle wax to the bowl and allow the heat to melt it. Carefully remove the bowl and repeat this process with the second bowl and the red candle wax.

As it cools, add three drops of lavender oil to the pink wax, and three drops of rose oil to the red wax. Wait until both waxes are cool enough to handle, then mould the pink wax into a small human figure. Do the same with the red wax. Now take the sprig of lavender and place it between the two figures. Squash them together as if they're both embracing the lavender. Light a match and carefully hold it against the two figures to melt them slightly together so they stay attached.

The figures represent you and your summer soulmate. Carry them in your pocket and you'll meet someone special very soon.

Lemon banishment spell

In folklore and magical traditions, lemons have long been prized for their purifying and protective properties. They are said to ward off evil and repel negativity. This spell harnesses the lemon's natural citrus power to neutralize the influence of someone who spreads harm or malice. For best results, cast it during a waning-moon phase.

YOU WILL NEED *a lemon, a knife, a photo of the person you want to banish, 11 silver pins, a black candle and matches.*

Cut the lemon into two halves and pin the photo of the person you want to banish to one half. Discard the other half. Divide your candle into nine equal parts by scoring it with a pin. Light the candle and, while thinking about the person who has been horrible to you, stick another pin into the lemon half with the photo.

Keep an eye on the candle as it burns down. Every time a segment burns away, place another pin into the lemon, remembering to focus on the hateful person and sending karma back to them.

Repeat this for every segment that burns down, until the candle has burned down completely.

Once the candle has burned away, take the lemon half with the photo and pins and discard it in the trash somewhere away from your home.

♥ Quartz summer love circle spell

This spell harnesses the high energy of the season to attract romance, using candlelight and rose quartz to focus your intention. For best results, cast this spell on a Friday.

YOU WILL NEED *a pink candle, 4 pink tealight candles, 4 small pieces of rose quartz crystal and matches.*

Place the pink candle in the centre of a table or desk, then arrange the four tealight candles around it. Now place one piece of rose quartz next to each tealight candle. Light the long pink candle first, followed by the four tealight candles. Say the following words:

'By the candlelight power, I allow you to light the way for love to come knocking at my door. By the candlelight power, I trust in you to bring me my ideal mate. By the candlelight power, I ask that you bring only good and positive people into my life. This is my request; so mote it be.'

Wave your dominant hand above the flame of the long pink candle, followed by each of the tealight candles (careful not to burn your hand). Allow the candles to burn down safely. As each tealight burns away, pick up the rose quartz next to it and place it in your pocket (or a safe place).

Clear away the spell and carry the four rose quartz crystals with you for the next 28 days.

♥ Soul sisters bonding spell

Summer is a season of warmth, laughter and shared moments, perfect for celebrating the bonds of friendship. This spell strengthens connections between friends and creates lasting memories. Cast on a sunny day with your closest friends.

YOU WILL NEED *a green outside space, a picnic blanket, picnic foods and daisies (or buttercups or other small flowers with long stems).*

Find a nice quiet area where you can set up your picnic with your friends. Sit together in a circle and begin picking daisies or other flowers. Make sure you pick flowers that have a long stem. As you pick a flower, pass it to the person on your right. When you have 13 flowers each, start to make daisy chains together. Thread one flower into the other, then pass the chain you're holding to the person on your right to add another flower. The person on your left will pass you their chain to add to, and so on.

When each of you has used up your 13 flowers, tie each chain into a flower crown. You should have enough for everyone. Place the flower crown you're holding on the head of the person to your right, then all say the following words:

'Soul sister, sister soul, together we celebrate the love that we hold. Together, forever, forever will be, the soul sisters, you and me.'

Flight safety spell

Travel can stir up nerves, but magic offers both comfort and protection. This spell calls upon Algiz, the rune of shielding and safety, to guard you on your journey. Cast it on the day you fly.

YOU WILL NEED *a black pen and a lemon balm leaf.*

Draw the Algiz rune (see reference image below) on to the lemon balm leaf and place it in your pocket. If you feel nervous, take out the leaf and smell it.

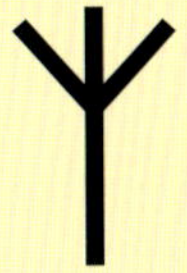

Solar shield spell

This spell, performed at the beach or in any sunny spot, draws upon the goddess Sol's radiant energy (see page 105) to shield and recharge your spirit.

YOU WILL NEED *a sunny day, a sandy beach (or any sunny spot with a patch of dirt) and a stick or wand.*

Find a quiet spot where you won't be disturbed. Draw a circle in the sand or dirt with your stick or wand, big enough for you to stand in. Stand inside the circle, facing the sun.

Close your eyes and raise your arms. Say the following words:

'By the power of Sol, may your rays warm and protect my soul. May your bright energy infuse my being. May your joy bathe my spirit. I give thanks to you. So mote it be.'

Stay in the circle until you feel rejuvenated.

Summer travel prosperity spell

Summer is a time for adventure, travel and making memories, but a little extra money can make your holiday even brighter. This spell draws abundance to you so you can fully enjoy your summer getaway. For best results, cast during a new-moon phase.

YOU WILL NEED *a bank note, your usual perfume and a sprig of dried lavender.*

Spray the bank note with your perfume, then pinch eight lavender seeds from the sprig and place them on the bank note. Fold it three times and place it in your wallet. Unexpected spending money will come to you soon.

Beach bag shield spell

Summer days at the beach are meant for fun and relaxation, not worrying about lost or stolen items. This spell will help safeguard your valuables while you enjoy the sun, sand and surf. Cast it the morning before you head out for a worry-free beach day.

YOU WILL NEED *your beach bag, bug-repellent spray and paper towels (or bug-repellent wipes), a summer rose (with a thorny stem) and a pair of scissors or secateurs.*

Empty your beach bag of any contents. Spray with bug-repellent spray, then use a paper towel to clean inside and outside the bag (or use a bug-repellent wipe). Allow a few minutes for it to dry, then pack your bag, adding only what you need to take to the beach with you. Don't put unnecessary items in there, and keep cash to a minimum.

Choose a summer rose, making sure the stem is long and has thorns on it. Spray a paper tower with bug-repellent spray (or take out a bug-repellent wipe) and lay it on a flat surface. Carefully cut all the thorns from the rose stem and catch them in the paper towel or wipe. Add a couple of rose petals on top.

Fold up the paper towel or wipe to secure its contents and place this in your beach bag. Finally, close your bag and wave your dominant hand over it as you visualize it being protected by a white light.

Love attraction oil spell

Summer's radiant energy is perfect for drawing love into your life. This spell calls upon Aphrodite, the goddess of love and beauty, to amplify romantic attraction. For best results, cast it on a Friday night.

YOU WILL NEED *6 teaspoons almond oil, 3 drops of jasmine essential oil, 3 drops of rose essential oil, 3 drops of gardenia essential oil, 3 drops of tuberose essential oil, a small bowl, a stick or wand, a pink candle and matches.*

Combine the almond oil and essential oils in the bowl and stir with your stick or wand. Anoint the pink candle with the oil by using your fingers to spread it all over the candle, then place it in a candle holder and light it. Set the intention that you are sending a request out to the universe for love to come and find you.

Say the following words as you dab some of the oil on your neck, wrists and inner elbows:

'I call to the love deity Aphrodite to say I am ready now to find love. May you send my attraction out into the universe to be caught by a worthy soul. So be it.'

Allow the candle to safely burn down and keep the oil for future use (it will last three months). You will begin to receive more romantic attention within a couple of days.

Summer harmony spell

Summer's long, bright days bring more social gatherings and opportunities to connect, but also more chances for miscommunication. This spell restores harmony and mends relationships, helping you resolve conflicts swiftly. For best results, cast it on a Monday.

YOU WILL NEED *2 orange candles, matches, still spring water, a glass tumbler, 6 rose petals and rose essential oil.*

Light both candles. The first represents you and the second represents the other person. Pour the spring water into the tumbler and add the rose petals and three drops of rose oil. Place the tumbler between the candles and say:

'Iris, the goddess of communication, bring peace and harmony between me and (name). May we settle our differences and be happy to respect one another's valid opinions and thoughts. So mote it be.'

Allow the candles to burn down safely, then take the rose water and sprinkle it and the rose petals outside of your home. Peace will soon be restored between the two of you.

Protective bubble spell

Summer is a time of activity and travel, and so you may spend some time away from loved ones. This spell surrounds those you care about with a magical protective bubble, keeping them safe and shielded from negative forces. For best results, cast it on a Saturday.

YOU WILL NEED *an empty jar with a lid, an incense stick, matches, several small strips of paper, a pen, Himalayan salt, dried basil, ground cinnamon and dried mugwort.*

Begin the spell by cleansing the jar. To do this, light your incense stick and blow it out so that it smokes. Place the incense stick in the jar and allow the smoke to waft inside.

On the strips of paper, write the names of the people you wish to protect in a protective bubble. Use one strip of paper for each name.

Remove the incense stick and pour a layer of salt into the bottom of the jar, followed by a pinch each of basil, cinnamon and mugwort (if you can't find these ingredients, use your favourite herbs and spices instead). Now add the strips of paper to the jar and place the lid on it. Shake the jar and say:

'We are protected from negative energy or harmful attacks. May only peace, love and light find its way into our lives. So mote it be.'

Keep the jar on a sunny windowsill and shake it up whenever you remember to keep the protective bubble around you and your loved ones.

Cucumber self-care ritual

Cucumbers are refreshing for both body and spirit; they are celebrated in folklore for their healing and calming properties and are rich in antioxidants.

YOU WILL NEED *a cucumber, a knife and a freezer bag.*

Slice the cucumber and keep the fresh slices in a freezer bag in the refrigerator. Use in self-care rituals as you wish: place them over tired eyes, blend into cooling smoothies or include them in spells that nurture your energy and wellbeing.

Summer party blessing

Summer is a time for celebration. This spell channels the vibrant energy of the season to ensure your party runs smoothly, fostering fun, laughter and joy. For best results, cast this spell on the Saturday before your party date.

YOU WILL NEED *a silver knife, fork and spoon for each partygoer, yellow flowers, yellow ribbon, a yellow candle and matches.*

Gather a silver knife, fork and spoon together and place a yellow flower with them, then tie them all together with the yellow ribbon. Repeat this for however many people are attending the party.

Place the cutlery bundles together in the centre of the party table, along with the yellow candle. Light the candle and say the following words:

'Here's the party, here comes the fun,
fill this room with the brightest sun.
May we all have a ball,
come forth one and all!'

Allow the candle to safely burn down. Lay one bunch of cutlery per place setting for your guests to use. If you're having a finger-buffet, you can substitute the cutlery bunches for serving utensils.

Summer travel safety spell

This spell creates a protective travel bracelet to help ensure that your journeys go smoothly and safely. For best results, cast during a new-moon phase before your trip.

YOU WILL NEED *embroidery thread in gold, green and red, and a silver charm.*

Take the three lengths of embroidery thread and tie them together in a knot at one end. Plait the three cords as you chant, 'Safe' over and over until the plait is complete. Add the charm to the bracelet and wear whenever you have to travel.

Lavender love baking charm

Lavender is known for its power to attract passion and affection. This magical baking spell uses the sweet scent and energy of this summertime herb to draw love into your life. For best results, cast it on a Friday night.

YOU WILL NEED *a baking sheet, baking paper, a purple candle, matches, 225g (1 cup) softened butter, 150g (¾ cup) caster sugar, a pinch of salt, a mixing bowl, ½ teaspoon vanilla extract, 1 egg, 270g (2 cups) plain flour, 2 teaspoons dried lavender flowers, a rolling pin, a heart-shaped cookie cutter and lavender ribbon.*

Preheat the oven to 150°C (300°F/ gas mark 2) and line the baking sheet with baking paper.

Light the purple candle. Mix together the butter, sugar and salt in a mixing bowl, then add the vanilla extract and egg. Stir in the flour and dried lavender. As you mix, keep saying the following words:

'I mix and mix and mix this up,
to bring to me lots of luck,
in finding someone close to me,
so that I will become we.
So mote it be.'

Roll out the cookie dough and use the cookie cutter to cut out heart shapes. Arrange the cookies on the prepared baking sheet and chill in the fridge for 5 minutes. Once chilled, transfer to the oven and bake for 20 minutes.

Once the cookies have baked, allow them to cool, then tie a lavender ribbon around each one and keep them in an airtight container for up to a week. Allow your candle to safely burn down and eat one cookie at midnight to set the spell in motion.

Seashell release spell

In folklore, seashells have long been seen as symbols of protection and safe passage, making them powerful tools for release. For best results, perform this during a waning-moon phase.

YOU WILL NEED *a seashell, a pencil and the sea.*

Wash any residual sand off the shell, then use the pencil to write on the shell what it is you wish to banish. Go to the sea and stand with your back to the surf.

Hold the shell in your hand and say:

'By the power of nature, by the power of the sea,
I ask you to take this from me.
By the power of the storm, by the power of the waves,
take this away to the darkest caves.
So be it.'

Throw the shell over your shoulder and into the sea. The ocean will carry away your troubles.

Lemon shield spell

Sometimes affection is unwanted, and summer's warmth can attract admirers who don't take a hint. This spell clears your space of unwanted attention. For best results, cast during a waning-moon phase.

YOU WILL NEED *a black pen, paper, a lemon, a knife, 13 cloves, a pinch of salt and something belonging to the pest (optional).*

Using the black pen, write the name of the person who has been bothering you on the paper. Cut the lemon in half and push the paper into the fleshy part of one half of the lemon. Place the cloves on top of that lemon half, and sprinkle with a pinch of salt. Place the other lemon half on top so that it looks like a full lemon again.

If you have something belonging to the perpetrator, such as an item of clothing, place the lemon on top of it. Say the following words:

'Your time is up, I've been nice,
but now you have to go.
No longer will you bother me
or disturb my flow.
So mote it be.'

Keep the lemon together and place it by your front door. Leave it there until it shrivels up, then throw it away. Dispose of any items belonging to the person so that their energy isn't hanging around.

Social energy renewal spell

This spell helps recharge your 'social battery', leaving you refreshed and ready to enjoy the warmer weather. Cast it anytime you feel socially drained.

YOU WILL NEED *seasonal fresh fruits and berries, a blender, a pinch of salt, 1 teaspoon lemon juice, 3 mint leaves, a few ice cubes and a tall glass.*

Wash and chop all your fruit and place it in your blender. Add a pinch of salt, followed by the lemon juice. Add the ice cubes and mint leaves, and blend until all the ingredients have mixed thoroughly. Pour your drink into a tall glass and allow it to settle. Say the following words:

'By the power of nature, I ask that you bring to me the energy from the four corners of the earth. May I be infused with strength and vigour from this day forth, so that I can be renewed once again. Thank you. So mote it be.'

Quietly sip your drink while visualizing your social battery filling back up, just as your phone does when it needs recharging. Don't rush the process. Before you know it, you'll be back on top form.

♥ Strawberry love spell

At this time of year, fruits are at their ripest and nature offers its sweetest gifts. This fruity spell restores the bond between you and your romantic partner. For best results, cast it on a Friday night.

YOU WILL NEED *3 large strawberries, a bowl, a squeeze of lemon juice, 3 drops of rose water, a silver spoon, a pink candle, matches and your partner.*

Remove the stalks from the strawberries and place the berries in a bowl. Add the lemon juice and rose water, and mash it all together with the back of the spoon. Allow the mixture to settle for a minute or two while you light the candle and turn out any electrical lighting.

Sit cross-legged with your partner, facing each other. Dip your finger into the mixture and mark the third-eye chakra (the point between the eyebrows) on your partner. Then allow them to do the same to you. Next dip your finger into the mixture and mark both cheeks and the chin on your partner's face, then allow them to do the same to you. Both repeat the following words:

'I give to you my love, my soul,
the fruits from nature fill this bowl.
I give to you my love, my heart,
from here on, our fresh start.'

Allow the candle to safely burn down before washing the mixture from your faces. You can now dispose of any leftover mixture. Your love will be restored.

★ Sand manifestation spell

This spell uses sand to physically manifest your dreams and connect your intentions with the flow of the tide. For best results, cast this spell on a Monday.

YOU WILL NEED *a sandy beach and a stick or wand.*

Think about what it is that you would like in your life right now, and spend some time visualizing how you will feel once it comes your way. Try to conjure up the feelings of opening an email to good news or receiving a phone call confirming you have achieved what you most desire. This is the most important part of manifesting magic - you have to really feel the results.

Find a quiet part of the beach and draw something that symbolizes your wish in the sand. For example, if you are looking for a new home, draw a house. If you are looking for love, draw a heart. Look at your drawing and say the following words:

'By the power of the earth, wind, fire and water, I ask that you grant me this wish and bring forth ideas and opportunities to make it reality. So mote it be.'

Walk away from the sand and allow Mother Nature to work her magic for you.

Nettle karma spell

This spell harnesses the stinging nettle, a plant known in folklore for protection and returning harmful energy, to send back ill-will. For best results, cast this spell during a full-moon phase.

YOU WILL NEED *gloves, stinging nettles, 2 jugs, boiling water, a pen, paper, a sieve or strainer and a clear water bottle with lid.*

Wearing gloves, pick a handful of stinging nettles and place them in a jug. Pour in the boiling water and leave the nettles to steep in the water for ten minutes. While you're waiting, sit and write the name or names of the person or people who have disrespected you or been mean to you.

Strain the nettle water into the second jug and, once it's cool, pour it into the water bottle. Place the paper into the bottle, close it and shake vigorously. Visualize the person or people getting payback for the way they have treated you.

Place the bottle somewhere you will see it every day, and shake it every time you pass by. By the time the paper has dissolved completely, the spell will have worked.

Summer travel blessing

This spell calls on Abeona, the Roman goddess of journeys; Adiona, the Roman goddess of safe return; and the Three Graces, often considered to be protectors of safe travel. It invites protection on your journeys, ensuring your holidays are safe and memorable. Cast this spell on the day you start your travels.

YOU WILL NEED *an A4 piece of paper, a pen, an orange tealight candle, a green tealight candle, a blue tealight candle, a white tealight candle and matches.*

Place the paper in landscape orientation on a table or desk where it won't be disturbed. In the middle of the paper, draw the mode of transport you will be using for your vacation. Draw a pentagram (see reference image on right) in the bottom left corner of the paper, and repeat in the bottom right corner.

Place the four tealights in a line on top of the paper (in any order) and light all four. Say the following words:

'By the power of Abeona, watch over me/us as I/we travel. By the power of Adiona, ensure a safe return. And by the power of the Three Graces, give me/us joy, merriment and good cheer. So mote it be.'

Allow the candles to safely burn down, then fold the paper into three and keep it with your travel documents.

♥ Seven-day candle love spell

This powerful seven-day candle spell helps you to cultivate self-love and confidence, then channel your energy outward to attract the right partner. For best results, begin this spell on a Friday.

YOU WILL NEED *7 pink candles, a sharp knife and matches.*

This spell is designed to be done on seven consecutive evenings. Take the first pink candle and carve a heart shape into the middle of the shaft, then carve your first initial into the heart. This is to remind you that you are loveable. Light the candle and say the following words:

'I matter. I am OK just as I am.
I am loveable.'

Allow the candle to safely burn down. Repeat this process for the next two days, preferably at the same time each night.

On the fourth day, take the fourth candle and this time engrave the candle with a circle with a question mark in the middle of it. Light the candle and say the following words:

'I send my unique energy out for all to see.
May you bring someone perfect back to me.'

Allow the candle to safely burn down. Repeat this process over the next three days with the remaining candles, until all seven candles have burned away.

Within seven weeks, you will meet someone new.

♥ Summer wedding broom blessing

Brooms have long been a symbol of domestic harmony in witchcraft. This summer wedding broom spell harnesses that power to bless a union – whether it's your own wedding or someone else's. Cast this spell the day after the wedding.

YOU WILL NEED *a witch's broom (see page 24 for how to make your own), flowers from the bridal bouquet, sprigs of rosemary, bay leaves, sprigs of elderflower, sprigs of lavender, sprigs of sage, blue ribbon, pink ribbon, green ribbon, orange ribbon, a glue gun and glue, and rose essential oil.*

The day after the wedding, take your broom and begin by putting some of the flowers from the bridal bouquet into the bristles. Next add the rosemary, bay leaves, elderflower, lavender and sage.

Wrap the coloured ribbons down the handle of the broom (you may need some glue to hold them in place). Finally, sprinkle the bristles of the broom with rose oil.

Lay the broom on the floor and, holding your spouse's hand, jump over it three times. Keep your broom in your new home. If you are making the broom for someone else, have the married couple jump over it three times and keep it in their home.

As a side note: if you want to get married, place a witch's broom on the floor and jump over it nine times. Legend says that you will be proposed to within the year.

Summer baby blessing

The arrival of a new baby is a time of hope and new beginnings. This gentle blessing can be used to bless a child with a life full of joy and strength.

YOU WILL NEED *a baby!*

Simply hold the baby in your arms and say:

'May the sun bring you energy. May the moon restore you at night. May the rain wash away your worries. May the breeze blow new strength into your being. May you walk gently through life.'

Threshold protection spray

Warm weather can bring unwanted pests, both in insect and human form. This simple magical spray uses protective and repellent herbs and spices to keep your space safe and your energy undisturbed.

YOU WILL NEED *a pinch of ground black pepper, a pinch of cayenne pepper, a pinch of salt, a pinch of dried sage, a pinch of dried garlic, a clean spray bottle and spring water.*

Add the black pepper, cayenne, salt, sage and garlic to your spray bottle. Top up with spring water and shake well. Spray across the threshold of your doorway.

Sand & sea cleansing spell

This spell works with the natural flow of the tide, allowing the ocean to carry away stagnant energy and make room for new opportunities or experiences. For best results, cast in the morning.

YOU WILL NEED *a sandy beach and a stick.*

Go to the beach first thing in the morning when it's quiet and you can be alone. Move as close to the ocean as you can and think about what it is you wish to get rid of – to draw a line under. Now, use the stick to draw a horizontal line in the wet sand. Write your initial above the line, then underneath the line write the first initial of the person or situation you wish to eliminate from your life.

Next, draw a cross through both letters in the sand, then stamp your bare feet on top to mess up the sand. Walk away and don't look back. As the tide comes in, it will take away the situation or the person you no longer need in your life.

Summer prosperity tea spell

This tea spell harnesses the energy of sun-filled days to attract prosperity into your life, whether for a new project, a career opportunity or a well-deserved holiday. For best results, cast this spell on a sunny Sunday morning.

YOU WILL NEED *water, a saucepan, a handful of mint leaves, a bay leaf, a handful of lemon balm leaves, a sprig of lavender, a handful of chamomile flowers, a sieve or strainer and your favourite mug.*

Boil your water in a saucepan on the stove, then add all the herbs and flowers. Simmer for five minutes, then take off the heat and allow to brew for ten minutes more.

Strain the liquid into your favourite mug – if you make too much, you can decant the rest into a glass bottle for use at another time (it will keep in the fridge for up to a week). Dispose of the plants in the compost. Hold the mug in your hands and repeat the following three times before sipping your tea.

'As I sip this tea, I bring to me, wonderful times of prosperity.'

Sip your drink throughout the day.

Summer career spell

Summer is a season of growth and opportunity, making it the perfect time to welcome new work, learning experiences or career advancements. This spell aligns your vibration with the energy of ambition and success, helping to open the right doors for you.

YOU WILL NEED *an orange candle, matches, white paper and an orange pen.*

Light your candle and place it in front of you on a table or desk. Clear your mind as you take your piece of paper and write at the top what you are hoping to achieve. Underneath, write down why you want it. Is it so you can earn more? Is it because you want to better yourself? Are you looking at starting a new career? Below this, write:

'Demeter, I ask you to take these words and manifest them into being.'

Now draw the triple moon symbol (see reference image below).

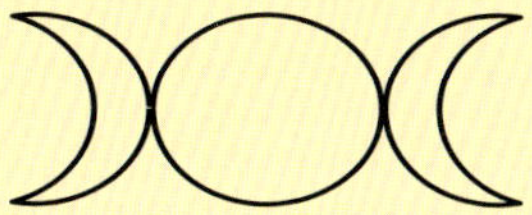

Drop three drops of orange candle wax on to the page, then blow the candle out. Keep the paper somewhere safe until your spell manifests.

Red knot release spell

The colour red has long been associated with power and protection in magical traditions. This quick, focused spell is perfect for banishing someone or something from your life.

YOU WILL NEED *a length of red cord or embroidery thread.*

Visualize the person, situation or habit you wish to remove from your life. Hold the cord in your hands and tie a knot at its centre, focusing all your intentions on banishing what no longer serves you. Place the cord in a dark, undisturbed place and leave it until your intention manifests.

Room cleansing spell

Homes can absorb and hold on to stagnant or negative energy, making it hard to relax or feel at peace. This quick home cleanse helps refresh the energy of any room.

YOU WILL NEED *salt.*

Clean the room thoroughly, and then place 1 teaspoon of salt in each corner of the room. If the energy of the room starts to feel 'off' again at a later date, clear the old salt and replace it with new.

Prosperity bloom spell

Abundance can be nurtured, just like a summer garden. This simple spell uses the natural growth of a plant to attract prosperity into your life. For best results, cast this spell on a Monday morning.

YOU WILL NEED *a summer flowering plant, a plant pot, compost, a silver coin and water.*

Plant your flowering plant in the plant pot, then push a silver coin into the soil with it. Water well. As your flower grows, so will your income.

Summer soul-purpose ritual spell

This spell reconnects you with your passions and life purpose by facilitating reflection and grounding you in nature. It's perfect for summer days when the world feels alive and full of possibility. For best results, cast on a sunny day.

YOU WILL NEED *a notebook, a pen, wildflowers and sticky tape.*

Find a meadow or an area with greenery. Sit down and take your shoes and socks off so you can feel the earth beneath your feet. Close your eyes and visualize yourself being connected to the earth. Imagine that your feet are growing roots into the ground.

Open your notebook and think about all the things that you enjoy doing, such as reading, walking, learning etc. Whatever gives you a buzz, write it down. By doing this, you are providing the cosmos with information about where your real purpose lies.

When you're happy with what you've written, look for some wildflowers and stick these into your notebook on the page where you've just written what brings you joy. You can now return to your home knowing that the universe will be working to send you information about what your purpose here on Earth is.

Bell cleansing spell

Sound healing is an ancient practice used to clear stagnant or negative energy. This spell is especially useful when your energy feels 'off' but you can't identify the cause.

YOU WILL NEED *a small bell.*

Ring the bell at different points around your body, and then in every room in your home. This will change the frequency of the vibrations surrounding you, and negative energy will quickly disappear.

Summer success spell

This spell welcomes clarity, confidence and positive outcomes. For best results, cast this spell on a Thursday evening.

YOU WILL NEED *a yellow tealight candle, a blue tealight candle, an orange tealight candle, matches, paper, a pen, your favourite incense, a pinch of ground cinnamon, a pinch of ground ginger, a pinch of salt and a paper bag.*

Light your three candles in any order, then sit with your paper and pen and write down in detail what it will mean to achieve the success you are hoping for.

When you've finished, light the incense stick and let the smoke waft over the paper. Scatter the cinnamon, ginger and salt on to the paper, then fold three times and place it in the paper bag.

Fold down the top of the paper bag and seal it by dripping a drop of candle wax from each candle on to the seam. Now place the three candles on top of the paper bag until they safely burn away. Keep the paper bag with your important documents and have faith that you will achieve success.

Quick money charm

This simple spell uses everyday kitchen ingredients to draw financial abundance into your life.

YOU WILL NEED *a pinch of ground coffee, a pinch of ground cinnamon powder and a pinch of salt.*

Place the coffee, cinnamon and salt in the palm of your non-dominant hand and rub your hands together. Repeat the words 'I attract wealth' 13 times as you rub, then wash your hands under warm water to release the spell. Unexpected money will soon come your way.

Lammas cleansing ritual

Lammas marks the first harvest and is a moment to pause, reflect and give thanks. It is a powerful time for shedding what no longer serves you so you have space to welcome abundance. For best results, cast this spell on Lammas.

YOU WILL NEED *an apple corer, 2 large apples, a knife, 6 sprigs of rosemary, 6 bay leaves, 6 mint leaves, silver pins, 2 white candles and matches.*

Use the apple corer to remove the core from each apple so that you are left with a hole in each one. Carve a pentagram (a five-pointed star within a circle, see page 124) into the skin of each apple, then attach three each of the rosemary sprigs, mint leaves and bay leaves to each apple with the silver pins. When you're happy with your decorating, place a candle in the hole of each apple and light them both. Say the following:

'On this special day, I call forth all the gods and goddesses to thank them for helping me so far this year. I ask that you cleanse my mind, body and spirit, my home, my surroundings and my life, so that I can go forth into the future feeling rejuvenated. Thank you. So mote it be.'

Allow the candles to burn down safely. While you are waiting, clean your home and tidy your desk, or anywhere you spend a lot of time. Once the candles have burned away, you can dispose of the apples.

Lammas crystal manifestation spell

Lammas is a moment to celebrate abundance while calling in blessings for the months ahead. Creating a crystal mandala during this Sabbat acts as a powerful amplifier of these fortuitous energies. Cast this spell on Lammas.

YOU WILL NEED *4 sprigs of rosemary, 4 large white quartz crystals, 4 small crystals of your choice, 1 large crystal of your choice and 4 summer flowers of your choice.*

Find an outside area where you won't be disturbed. Lay the four sprigs of rosemary on the ground so that one points north, one east, one south and one west. This represents earth, wind, fire and water.

Above each sprig, place a large white quartz crystal to ignite the spell's power. Between each sprig, place a smaller crystal of your choice. Place a flower above each sprig. Finally, hold the large crystal in your cupped hands and repeat the following words:

'I call upon all gods and goddesses on this Sabbat of Lammas. I celebrate you and bring you these gifts of nature. May you bring to me all that I need in this life and bless me with your power. So mote it be.'

Gently blow your intentions into your hands, then place the crystal you were holding in the centre of your mandala. Leave the mandala in place for a full 28 days, then gather up your crystals and re-cleanse them with running water. Return the rosemary and flowers to Mother Nature.

Bread of abundance spell

Lammas celebrates the gifts of the earth. This bread spell channels gratitude and abundance into your life. For best results, perform on or around Lammas.

YOU WILL NEED *ingredients for your favourite bread recipe, rosemary (optional), a loaf tin and a knife or athame.*

Prepare the bread dough according to your favourite recipe, adding rosemary for extra abundance if you wish. As you knead the dough, visualize the energy of abundance being sent into the mixture. Once your loaf has proved, place it in a loaf tin. Use your knife or athame to carve the shape of a piece of corn into the top of the loaf (this represents the harvest) then bake it according to your recipe and allow to cool.

Prior to eating the bread, hold your hand over the loaf and say:

'I bless this bread before me to bring abundance to all who eat it. May it nourish our bodies, our spirits and our souls, and bring all that we need in life. So mote it be.'

Corn doll guardian spell

Corn dolls, also called corn mothers, were traditionally made from the last sheaf of grain at harvest. They were believed to embody the spirit of the harvest, offering protection, fertility and prosperity to the household.

YOU WILL NEED *corn husks or straw, water, scissors, natural twine and white ribbon.*

Spray corn husks or straw with a little water to make them more pliable. Bundle a few stems together to form the body of the doll, and secure with some twine. Form two arms and two legs and attach these to the body with twine, then bend one more stem into a circle, and attach this to the neck of the body to create a head. Finally, tie a white ribbon around the neck of the corn doll. To welcome your corn doll, say the following:

'Greetings, blessed one. I bring life to you in return for protection and guidance in all that I do and all that I am. May we journey together in safety.'

Name your corn doll and carry her with you for protection and guidance.

Golden grain prosperity spell

Lammas celebrates abundance and gratitude for the earth's bounty. This spell helps you align with prosperity and manifest your needs. For best results, perform this spell on or around Lammas.

YOU WILL NEED *a green candle, matches, a bowl of grain, rice or corn, paper and a green pen.*

Sit down at your altar or in a quiet space. Light the green candle and bless the bowl of grains by saying thank you to Mother Nature for providing you with them. Think about what you need to make your life easier and abundant.

Write this down on the paper in green ink. When you've finished writing, fold the paper into three and bury it in the bowl of grains. Hold the bowl in your hands and say:

'Grains of the earth, may the harvest bring me plenty and may my life be blessed with abundance, good fortune and prosperity. So be it.'

Leave the bowl on a sunny windowsill for seven days, then remove the paper and scatter the grains outside to return them to nature.

Lammas harvest blessing

Lammas is a time to give thanks for nourishment, growth and community. A foraged meal is a beautiful way to celebrate this Sabbat.

YOU WILL NEED *a basket, an outside space for foraging and other ingredients.*

Spend the morning foraging responsibly for wild foods such as berries, greens, herbs or mushrooms. Always check the safety and edibility of the items you gather.

Take your foraged harvest home and combine the foods with other ingredients to prepare simple dishes such as berries in yogurt or wild herb bruschetta.

Take your food outside to enjoy, either alone or with loved ones. As you eat, pause to express gratitude for the turning of the year, the sun, the earth and the cycles of nature that sustain you.

Lammas fire purge spell

Lammas is not only a time for gratitude; it is also a turning point and a time for release. Using the purifying element of fire, this spell encourages you to release your burdens to the flames. Cast this spell outside on the evening of Lammas.

YOU WILL NEED *paper, a red pen, a fire pit or fireproof dish, matches and a handful of mixed herbs.*

Sit for a while and think about what it is you wish to banish from your life. This could be a person or a situation. Write it down in as much detail as possible using the red pen. Next, draw a big cross through what you've written.

If you're using a fire pit, light your fire. Hold the paper in your hand and say the following words:

'By the power of Sol, I call upon you to remove this from my life.
No longer will I suffer from harm or strife.
So mote it be.'

Light the paper and either throw it into the fire pit or drop it into your fireproof dish. Take the handful of herbs and throw them into the flames. Be mindful to not linger after the fire has gone out.

New project blessing

Summer's vibrant energy makes it the perfect time to launch a new venture. This spell calls upon Ra, the radiant sun god of ancient Egypt, who is represented by a falcon. By working with his solar energy, you infuse your project or business with the momentum it needs to take flight.

YOU WILL NEED *a piece of paper that relates to the project that you wish to bless (such as a business card, invoice or note of ideas), a printout or drawing of the Sun Tarot card, a hole-punch, yellow ribbon, a yellow tealight candle, matches and a pin.*

Place the paper relating to your project on top of the Sun Tarot card image. Use the hole-punch to make a hole at the bottom of the two items, then thread the yellow ribbon through both items and tie them together, leaving a long tail of ribbon.

Light the yellow tealight candle and place this on top of the combined items. Visualize your fledging business growing as you say the following words:

'By the power of Ra, ruler of all gods, I ask that you take my ideas with you and make them fly, so that they may manifest into reality. I give thanks; so mote it be.'

Allow the candle to safely burn away before pinning the combined items to a pinboard or a wall in your office, or wherever you usually work.

Tarot compass spell

This simple Tarot spell is designed to realign you with your inner compass. By working with the cards, you invite your intuition and the wisdom of the universe to gently guide you back on track. Cast any time you feel your life lacks direction.

YOU WILL NEED *a deck of Tarot cards with a booklet of meanings (unless you already know them) and a journal and pen (optional).*

Shuffle your Tarot deck while focusing on the following intention: 'Show me the way forward.' Draw three cards and lay them before you. Turn them over and read them left to right.

The cards represent the following:

1 – The Focal Point Card – reveals where your attention is most needed right now.
2 – The Receiving Card – shows what or who is coming in to support you.
3 – The Gift Card – uncovers how the universe will help you move ahead.

Take a few moments to sit with your cards. If you like, you can journal your thoughts, and let your intuition lead. The answers are already within you – you're simply uncovering them.

Forgiveness bath spell

The past can linger like a shadow. This ritual bath is designed to help you let go and step forward feeling lighter and renewed. For best results, cast during a waning-moon phase.

YOU WILL NEED *a bathtub, 1 teaspoon dried lavender, 1 teaspoon dried sage, 1 teaspoon ground cinnamon, 1 teaspoon mixed herbs, 3 mint leaves, a bay leaf, a pinch of salt, a small cloth bag, a white candle and matches.*

As you run a hot bath, combine all the dried herbs and spices in your cloth bag, then tie it shut. Light the white candle and throw the herb bag into the water. As you step into the bath, say the following words:

'I hereby forgive myself. I hereby forgive others. I am now free from the past, to live my life in the most wondrous way. I release the previous me. I release the previous pain. This is my wish; so mote it be.'

Submerge yourself in the water and visualize the ingredients releasing anything that has troubled you and healing you as they infuse the water. Stay in the bath until you feel released.

Repeat this spell every time you find yourself stuck thinking about the past.

Salt purification spell

Salt is a simple pantry item that has long been a cornerstone in magical practice, used in purifying and cleansing spells. This simple spell allows you to wash away stagnant energy and refresh your body and spirit, perfect after a busy summer week.

YOU WILL NEED *salt, a cleansing mitt or washcloth, a small bowl of water and a shower.*

Undress and tip a handful of salt on to your cleansing mitt or washcloth. Add a few drops of water to dampen the salt slightly. Gently scrub your body with the mitt or cloth, visualizing all negative energy, stress and fatigue being absorbed by the salt and washed away.

Rinse yourself thoroughly in the shower, imagining yourself refreshed, renewed and full of energy for the days ahead.

Opportunities spell

Lammas is all about exploring new opportunities, but sometimes we need a little help to recognize them and take that first step. This spell works to open new paths and invite positive opportunities into your life. For best results, cast this spell during a new-moon phase.

YOU WILL NEED *a white candle, matches, an old key (see note) and a length of red cord.*

Light the white candle and hold the key between the palms of your hands. Look into the candle flame and visualize powerful positive energy being infused into the key. Imagine everything that is possible is being absorbed by the key. Now say the following words:

'By the power of three, I infuse this key
with the power of all knowing.
By the power of three, I infuse this key
with the power of doors opening.
By the power of three, I infuse this key
with the power of opportunities.
With the power of three, I infuse this key
with the power of protection for me.
So mote it be.'

Continue visualizing sending your raw energy into the key. Next, carefully pass the key through the flame of the candle three times – be careful not to burn yourself. Finally, thread the key on to the red cord and tie it around your neck as a necklace. Wear it every day to open new doors and opportunities for yourself.

Note: If you don't have an old key, you can buy one at a market. If you use a key that hasn't belonged to you, wash it in salt water prior to casting this spell to get rid of any historical energy it might hold.

Cord-cutting candle ritual

Sometimes, certain people, habits or situations can drain your energy or hold you back. This spell is designed to banish what no longer serves you, freeing space for the new after Lammas. For best results, cast this spell during a waning-moon phase.

YOU WILL NEED *a fireproof plate, a black dinner candle, 5 silver pins, a length of black thread, 3 mint leaves, paper, a black pen and matches.*

Set your candle in its holder on a fireproof plate. Take one of the silver pins and push it through the top of the candle, close to the wick. Tie your black thread to the pin, then wind the rest of the thread around the shaft of the candle until it reaches the bottom. Secure the thread to bottom of the candle shaft with another pin.

Pin the three mint leaves on to the candle – one at the top, one in the middle and one at the bottom.

On the piece of paper, write down what it is that no longer serves you, and place this underneath the candle. Light the candle and say the following:

'By the power of one, the spell has begun.
By the power of two, I call to you.
By the power of three, send help to me.
No longer is this serving me.
I ask that you banish and bind
and release this from my mind.
So be it.'

Allow the candle to safely burn down. As the thread burns and the pins fall from the candle, your attachment to this person or situation is being severed.

Summer prosperity elixir

Mint is associated with prosperity and wealth. This spell allows you to harness that energy while enjoying a classic mojito, perfect for a sunny afternoon.

YOU WILL NEED *2 limes, a glass, 1 tablespoon caster sugar, a handful of fresh mint leaves (plus extra to decorate), plenty of ice, 50ml (3 tablespoons) rum (optional), soda water, a stirrer and a straw.*

Squeeze the limes into your glass, then add the sugar and stir until it dissolves. Add the mint leaves and muddle together. Fill the glass with plenty of ice, then pour in the rum (if using) and top up with soda water.

As you stir your drink, say the following words out loud:

'I ask you, prosperity gods, to bring to wealth my way. I ask that my debts are cleared, and money comes easily to me, and I have no financial stress from this day forth. So mote it be.'

Add a few mint leaves for decoration, then pop in a straw and enjoy your drink, knowing that once you have finished, you will have commanded the money gods to grant your wish.

★ Full-moon manifestation brew

The full moon is a time of heightened energy and manifestation. This ceremony harnesses its magic to invite abundance. For best results, perform in the evening during a full-moon phase.

YOU WILL NEED *milk, a saucepan, hot chocolate powder or cocoa, a pinch of ground turmeric, a pinch of ground cinnamon, 3 cloves, a pinch of salt, a wooden spoon, a strainer, a mug, incense and matches.*

Pour the milk into the saucepan and place over a medium heat to warm through, being careful not to let it boil. Add the chocolate powder or cocoa, along with the spices and salt. Stir with your wooden spoon and say the following words:

'By the power of Luna, I thank you for all your power. I ask that you infuse this magical drink with love, light and blessings aplenty. So mote it be.'

Close your eyes and ask your intuition to tell you what you need in your life right now. When you receive an answer, gently blow your intention into the pan.

Take the pan off the heat and strain the drink into a mug. Prior to drinking, light your incense and let the smoke drift over you. Now sit back and enjoy your magical full-moon drink. What you intended will soon be on its way.

Psychic enhancement spell

Every witch has psychic potential, and this spell helps you tune into yours by strengthening your connection with your spirit guides. For best results, cast it on a Sunday evening.

YOU WILL NEED *5 dried bay leaves, a notebook, a pen, a white candle, matches and a fireproof dish.*

The night before you cast the spell, place the bay leaves under your pillow. This may cause you to have vivid dreams, so keep a notebook beside your bed to record any dreams when you wake up.

The following night, light your candle and meditate on the flame for a few minutes. Ask your spirit guides to move forward to you to give you guidance and answers. Think of a question you would like to be answered, then place the bay leaves into the fireproof dish. Light the point of each leaf and concentrate on your question. Close your eyes. If the leaves begin to crackle or burn brightly, the answer is yes. If the leaves refuse to burn, then the answer is no.

This spell can take a bit of practice, so don't be despondent if it doesn't work the first time. The more you ask your guides to come forward, the more they will answer you. Once you've finished, safely discard the remnants of the bay leaves, then blow out the candle and keep it safe to use next time you cast this spell.

Magic summer candles

Candles are at the heart of many spells, calling forth the element of fire and amplifying your magic. By creating your own summer candle, you infuse it with personal and solar energy, making your spells more powerful.

YOU WILL NEED *soy candle wax, a heatproof bowl, a saucepan, yellow food colouring, your favourite essential oils, a wooden stirrer, an empty jar, a candle wick, a clothes peg and 3–4 small crystals.*

Place the soy wax in a heatproof bowl and set it over a saucepan of simmering water, making sure the bowl doesn't touch the water. Stir occasionally until the wax is fully melted.

Allow the wax to cool for a few minutes prior, then add the yellow food colouring and six drops each of your essential oils (add more if you want a more fragrant candle).

Stir, then pour the wax into the jar, placing the candle wick in the centre as you do so. You can use a clothes peg to hold the wick in place while the wax sets if needed. Just before the wax fully hardens, place the crystals on top. Leave your candle to set and cure for the next 24 hours.

You can use your homemade candle in spells and rituals that require fire.

Third-eye activation meditation

Summer's energy brings clarity and heightened perception. This simple meditation helps you open your third eye, enhancing intuition.

YOU WILL NEED *a quiet, grassy outside space and a coin (optional).*

Sit cross-legged on some grass to centre yourself and breathe in and out deeply. Visualize your third eye opening.

Remain like this for a minimum of ten minutes until you feel more open.

A good test to see if your third eye has been activated is to sit upright and place a coin of any denomination in the centre of your forehead. If the coin remains when you take your hand away, you have opened your third-eye chakra.

New-moon money-bowl spell

This money-bowl spell harnesses lunar energy to draw financial opportunities your way. For best results, cast this spell during a new-moon phase.

YOU WILL NEED *a glass bowl, filtered water, 3 silver coins, 3 gold floating candles, a handful of summer flower petals, matches and a jar.*

Fill the glass bowl with the filtered water. Place the silver coins into the bottom of the bowl, then place the gold candles on top of the water, followed by the petals. Light the candles as you visualize more money coming to you.

Bow your head and give thanks to the money gods, then allow the candles to burn away. Dispose of the water and petals, then dry the silver coins and place them in a jar on a sunny windowsill.

Whenever you have some spare silver coins, drop them into the jar to keep the magic going. When you have a few more coins in your jar, place three under your doormat and another three in your purse or wallet.

Summer intuition spell

Palo santo comes from the *Bursera graveolens* tree native to parts of South America. Traditionally, Indigenous peoples have used it in rituals for spiritual cleansing and connection with the sacred. This spell uses palo santo to open your intuitive side. Always source palo santo from reputable suppliers who harvest sustainably and support Indigenous communities. Use palo santo with gratitude and respect, acknowledging its cultural origins.

YOU WILL NEED *an ethically sourced palo santo stick, a candle and matches.*

Because palo santo is a natural product and there are no burning additives, you have to keep relighting it in order to retain the smoke. I suggest lighting a candle so that you can use this to relight the palo santo as needed.

Find an area where you can meditate in peace and quiet, and sit cross-legged on the floor. Light the candle and the palo santo stick, then blow out the palo santo flame. The palo santo stick will smoulder and produce a fragrant smoke.

Close your eyes and ask the Green Goddess (the feminine version of the Green Man) to open your intuitive side. Waft the smoke all over yourself, from the top of your head down to your toes. You may need to relight the stick. Imagine you're in a smoke shower with the smoke penetrating your skin.

After ten minutes, you can stop relighting the stick and allow it to extinguish itself naturally. Keep an eye on your dreams and record any intuitive thoughts you have during the day.

Summer blessing cards

In an age of instant messages, the personal touch of a handwritten note carries a unique kind of magic. This spell allows you to send good fortune to someone you care about. By crafting and blessing these cards, you create a tangible vessel of your love and intentions.

YOU WILL NEED *summer flowers, paper, heavy books, glue, a blank card and envelope, a pen, candle wax (optional) and a postage stamp.*

Pick some summer flowers with their stems and place them between two sheets of paper, then place in the middle of a heavy book. Place more books on top and leave for 48 hours so that the flowers dry out and are pressed flat.

Glue the dried flowers to the front of the card. On the inside of the card, write the following words on the left-hand side:

'Magic is everywhere...All you need to do is believe!'

Now write a personal message on the right-hand side, telling the person you are sending it to how much they mean to you, or anything else you would like them to know. Place the card in the envelope. If you like, you can seal it with wax; alternatively, draw a pentagram (a five-pointed star within a circle, see page 124) on the envelope as a seal. Send it by mail to the recipient. Once they receive it, they will also receive good luck or happy news.

Summer luck horseshoe charm

Horseshoes have long been symbols of luck and protection. There are many theories as to why horseshoes are considered lucky, including that blacksmiths were held in high regard by society, or that iron can ward off evil. This spell transforms simple craft items into a personal talisman, inviting positivity and luck into your space. This spell is particularly powerful after a planet has been in retrograde to get energies back to normal again.

YOU WILL NEED *a pen, a piece of thick card, scissors, glue and 8 small crystals or gemstones.*

Draw the shape of a horseshoe on your piece of card, making sure it's roughly the same size as a real horseshoe. Cut it out. Divide the horseshoe into eight equal segments and glue a small crystal or gemstone on to each segment, then write something that you desire underneath each crystal or gemstone.

When the glue has dried, stick your horseshoe above the door into your home (position it upright, so it looks like a 'U'). If you can't or don't want to do this, keep it safe somewhere where only you know about it. Your luck will soon improve.

New-moon clarity spell

Sometimes life feels confusing, and we need a little help to see things clearly. A new moon in summer is perfect for fresh beginnings, making it ideal for this clarity spell. For best results, cast in the evening during a new-moon phase.

YOU WILL NEED *a jar with a lid, spring water, a handful of lemon balm leaves and a pinch of salt.*

Fill the jar two-thirds full with spring water, then add the lemon balm and a pinch of salt. Place the lid on the jar and shake vigorously as you say:

'On this summer's moon, bring clarity back to me. May the darkness pass so that I find light once again. May the goddess Luna bless me with insight now. I give thanks as I ask this time to pass by.'

Leave the jar outside for one night, then pour the solution on the ground the next morning.

Daily gratitude ritual

Start your day by setting a positive tone and connecting with the universe's abundant energy so that you are in the right mindset for spellcasting.

Every day, before you get out of bed, say thank you for the fact you have woken up this morning. Say thank you for senses, for the roof over your head and the bed you've just slept in. Say 'thank you' seven times.

As you get out of bed and think about the day ahead, say the word 'please' seven times. This sends a message out to the universe to supply you with a good day. Then say 'thank you' again, seven more times. You will be amazed by how well your day goes.

Sunlight reset spell

We all have moments when we feel a little off-balance. Many traditions view the sun as a source of vitality and renewal, and this sunshine ritual can help realign energy and restore clarity. For best results, do this on a sunny day.

When you're next out in the summer sunlight, pause for a moment. Close your eyes, remove any sunglasses and tilt your face upwards, allowing the sun's glorious rays to penetrate your whole being. The sun will reactivate your pineal gland, producing melatonin, which will reset you and get you back on track. Do this as often as you can during the summer months.

★ Moonlight summer perfume

This spell infuses essential oils with the full moon's energy to create a fragrance uniquely attuned to the seasonal energy.

YOU WILL NEED *lemon essential oil, rose essential oil, mint essential oil, a 15ml (½fl oz) dark glass bottle with a lid, a funnel and moon water (see page 18).*

Add three drops each of the lemon, rose and mint essential oils to your glass bottle with the help of the funnel, then top up with your moon water to fill the bottle. Cover with the lid and place the bottle outside, preferably under moonlight, for one night.

The following morning, bring your bottle inside and give it a good shake to mix the oils with the water. Dab a drop or two of the scent you've made on to your temples, wrists, neck and inner elbows. The scent will attract magical opportunities towards you. Your scent will last for three months. Shake well every time you use it.

If you prefer a different scent, feel free to experiment with different essential oils, but always use moon water.

Summer chakra realignment spell

There are seven main chakras in your body (see list of chakras), and they can often get blocked, especially if you encounter negative energy. Carry out this spell anytime you feel 'off' in your mind or body.

YOU WILL NEED *lavender essential oil.*

To quickly clear any one of your chakras, put a drop of lavender oil on your index finger, then gently rub the oil on each chakra point. Allow the lavender oil to absorb into the skin. Within minutes, your chakra points will be reset, and you can go about your day.

THE SEVEN CHAKRAS

The Root Chakra – located at the base of the spine for survival.

The Sacral Chakra – located in the lower abdomen for creativity.

The Solar Plexus Chakra – located in the upper abdomen for confidence.

The Heart Chakra – located in the centre of the chest for compassion.

The Throat Chakra – located in the throat for communication.

The Third Eye Chakra – located between the eyebrows for intuition.

The Crown Chakra – located at the top of the head for spiritual connection.

Summer goddess intuition spell

This spell is designed to help you strengthen your intuition and psychic abilities by drawing on the radiant energy of the summer sun goddess, Sol, to illuminate the mind, reveal hidden truths and inspire insight.

YOU WILL NEED *a picture of the Norse goddess Sol, a yellow candle, matches, a moonstone crystal, a notebook and a pen.*

Perform this spell during a time when you won't be disturbed. Place the picture of Sol in front of the candle, then light the candle. Mentally ask Sol to come forward and help you to open your intuition. Using your non-dominant hand, hold the moonstone to the centre of your forehead, where your third-eye chakra is located. Close your eyes and slowly breathe in and out. Try to ignore any background noise as you visualize your third eye opening.

Continue to hold the moonstone to your forehead and keep your eyes closed. With your other hand, reach for the pen and begin writing anything that comes into your mind. This can take a little practice, but stay with it. You might start by writing down everything that you either feel, hear, see, sense or smell. Do this until your mind goes blank. You can now blow out the candle and put the crystal down.

It's important when you open your eyes again that you don't read what you have written straight away, because your body needs to readjust to the earthly world once more. Do something ordinary such as making a cup of coffee before returning to your notes. The more you do this spell, the more intuitive and psychic you will become.

Summer shadow-work spell

Personal growth involves acknowledging and embracing the aspects of ourselves we often overlook. This shadow-work spell uses sunlight to help you reflect, release and learn from your inner truths. For best results, perform on a sunny day.

YOU WILL NEED *a journal and a pen.*

Find a place to sit down outside. Make sure the sun is behind you, so that you see your shadow in front of you. Sit upright and place your journal on your lap. Look at your shadow and say the following words:

'My shadow self, I bring you forth so that I may reflect on my journey so far. I will not judge or be ashamed. I bring you forth so that I may learn lessons to be my higher self.'

Take a couple of deep breaths and close your eyes. Write down whatever comes into your mind. This might be words or images that you see in your mind, or full-sentence messages. Don't try to edit as you go; just write whatever comes up.

When you feel you have as many answers as you need for now, close your journal and open your eyes. Wait a full day before reflecting on what you have written.

Summer moon wish spell

This spell uses moon-charged water to symbolically let go of old patterns and embody the qualities you wish to cultivate. For best results, cast this spell in the evening during a full-moon phase.

YOU WILL NEED *a bottle of spring water, 2 clear glass tumblers, 2 sticky notes and a pen.*

The night before you cast this spell, put your bottle of water outside or on a windowsill from where the full moon is visible. This will charge the water inside.

To perform the spell, place the two glass tumblers next to each other. On one sticky note, write down what it is you wish to release from your current reality. Stick this on to the first tumbler. Now fill this tumbler to the top with your moon water.

Next, think about how you would prefer to be, and write this intention on the second sticky note – for example, 'I am now super confident'. Assume that once you have performed this spell, your intention is going to manifest. For this spell to work, it's very important to have faith.

When you feel ready, pour the water from the first tumbler into the second one and visualize what you wish to be released from disappearing, and being replaced by what you wish for. Drink the water from the second tumbler. Water picks up energy, and the energy from your intention is transferred to the water. Once you drink the water, you will have replaced resistance with power.

Summer home luck spell

This spell calls on the Wiccan deities Pan (Lord), who represents nature, and Hecate (Lady), who represents witchcraft. It uses herbs that flourish during the warmer months to create a charm that protects your doorway. For best results, cast on a Monday during a waxing-moon phase.

YOU WILL NEED *5 sprigs of rosemary, 5 sprigs of parsley, 5 sprigs of lavender and 1 metre (3 feet) of green ribbon.*

All the herbs need to be dried, so if they are fresh, dry them out by placing them in a warm oven or a cupboard. When they're dry, gather them all together into a bunch and tie them with the green ribbon, leaving a tail of the ribbon for hanging. Say the following words:

'Only good luck may pass through this house. Bad luck is not permitted. My Lord and Lady, encourage the flow of good luck to my home.'

Hang your lucky bunch of herbs above the doorway to your home. When it starts to look a bit tired, repeat the spell and replace the herbs with new ones. Your home will repel bad luck and only welcome in good.

Travelling luck talisman

This spell originates in Wales. It transforms a small pouch into a talisman of luck and happiness, perfect for your home, car or any other personal space. For best results, cast this spell during a waxing-moon phase.

YOU WILL NEED *a green candle, matches, a small piece of paper, a green pen, a stick of your favourite incense, 3 of your favourite crystals and a small pouch or bag.*

Light the green candle. Take your piece of paper and pen and write the word 'hapus' three times – this is the Welsh word for luck and happiness. Light the incense stick from the flame of the candle and waft the smoke over the paper, your pouch and the crystals you've chosen. Allow the incense stick to burn away before rolling up the piece of paper into a scroll and placing that and the crystals into the pouch.

Allow the candle to safely burn down, then hang your lucky bag above the doorway to your home. When you hit the road, take your lucky bag with you, and replace it in the doorway when you get home again. Luck will travel with you now.

White quartz renewal spell

Quartz has been revered for thousands of years for its energetic and healing properties. This spell uses the natural energy of white quartz to support physical, emotional and spiritual realignment. For best results, cast during a new-moon phase.

YOU WILL NEED *a white quartz crystal and meditation music.*

Begin by finding a time when you can sit quietly and not be disturbed. Wash your quartz crystal in running water to get rid of any negative energy it might have picked up, then dry it. Turn on some meditation music and sit or lie down. Make sure you're comfortable.

Start by holding the quartz between the palms of your hands. Keep holding it until it feels warm. This is a sign that the crystal is energizing. You might even feel it vibrating between your hands – this means that the energy the crystal is emitting is very powerful.

When you feel ready, think about the parts of you that need healing. If it's a physical pain, place the quartz on that part of your body. Visualize the frequencies from the crystal penetrating through your skin and absorbing the pain. If your pain is to do with your mental health, place the quartz in the centre of your forehead, where your third-eye chakra is situated. Breathe slowly as you visualize the crystal absorbing your negative thoughts.

Leave the crystal in place until you feel it has absorbed all the pain, then end the ritual.

Intuitive clarity ritual

Overthinking can cloud your mind and block your natural intuition. Meridians are the areas that regulate the flow of energy throughout the body. When these are out of line, it disturbs our natural energy. This simple grounding ritual releases anxiety and clears space for inner guidance.

The minute you start to overthink a situation, try holding the index finger on your left hand with your right hand. Hold it tightly for one minute. The meridians that are in your index finger are associated with the element of air, and are also connected to the gut, where anxiety and overthinking often affects us in the body. Repeat this anytime you feel anxious or are overthinking something. Within a few minutes, you will feel relaxed again.

Lime full-moon water spell

Infuse the cleansing energy of limes with the full moon's power to banish misfortune from your life. For best results, cast this spell overnight during a full-moon phase.

YOU WILL NEED *a lime, a knife and glass of water.*

Slice the lime and place the slices into a glass of water. Leave the glass outside under the full moon to energize. The following morning, bring the glass inside and place it under your bed. Say:

'Good energy is now restored. Negativity is no more.'

Leave the glass under your bed until the full moon disappears, then pour the lime and water away somewhere outside near your home.

Summer gratitude spell

This spell honours the growth that summer has brought you as you prepare for the next season. For best results, perform this spell outside, towards the end of August.

YOU WILL NEED *a yellow pen, a mirror, a sheet of paper, matches and a fireproof dish.*

With the yellow pen, draw a picture of the sun directly on to the mirror. Next, sit and write down on paper everything that you can think of, big and small, that you've achieved so far in your life. This could be anything from getting a job, to helping someone in need. Whatever comes into your mind, write it down. Don't be humble.

When you feel happy with your list, look into the mirror and recite the list out loud to your reflection. Finally, tell yourself you are amazing.

Set the list alight and drop it into the fireproof dish to safely burn and let the universe know what an incredible person you are.

AUTUMN

Autumn (or fall) is one of the most powerful and transformative seasons in the witch's year. The air grows crisp, the days shorten and nature begins its slow retreat into rest. This is the season of harvest and reflection: a time to gather the fruits of our labour and give thanks for what has come to pass, embracing change and preparing ourselves for the stillness of winter. In most of Europe, the autumn period typically begins in September and ends at the start of November. However, even if you live in a place without turning leaves, the feelings autumn evokes and encourages are the same: gratitude, purification and transformation.

Autumn festivals & celebrations

Mabon *(Autumn Equinox/Second Harvest Festival)*

Falling between 20 and 24 September, Mabon marks the balance of light and dark, when day and night are equal in length. It is known as the second harvest; while Lughnasadh is the time for harvesting the crops and grain, Mabon is the time for harvesting fruits and vegetables, such as apples and pumpkins.

Traditionally, this is a moment of balance and gratitude, a pause before the descent into winter. Witches celebrate Mabon by feasting, giving thanks, reflecting on the past months and setting intentions for the darker half of the year. It is also a time when many witches dedicate themselves to study, learning or deepening their practice.

Worshippers of Mabon believe that this is a time of reincarnation, and they give thanks and blessings to those who have passed over. As we start to approach Samhain, it is believed that the veil to the Underworld becomes thinner.

Samhain *(All Hallows' Eve/Halloween)*

On 31 October, witches celebrate Samhain (pronounced 'sow-inn'), one of the most important Sabbats of the year. Samhain marks the last of the eight Sabbats before the earth settles down into a deep sleep. The word itself means 'summer's end'; nature retreats to gain the energy it needs to come back to life in the spring. Those who don't follow the Wiccan faith still celebrate Samhain in the form of Halloween.

The celebration comes from the Gaelic and Celtic new year's festival, which was held on 1 November and was a time for paying respects to ancestors. This celebration was later adopted by Christians as All Saints' Day. Samhain is known as the time when the veil between the worlds of the living and the dead is thinnest.

At this time, witches honour ancestors and departed loved ones, lighting candles and practising divination spells. It is a festival of endings and beginnings, release and rebirth, and it carries immense transformative energy.

Autumn goddesses

Persephone

In Greek mythology, Persephone embodies the cycle of death and rebirth. Autumn marks her return to the Underworld, symbolizing descent, reflection and transformation. She is often invoked for guidance through periods of change and for help with embracing cycles of renewal.

Modron

A Welsh mother goddess associated with Mabon, Modron is linked to harvest, fertility and the turning of the year. She represents nurturing, balance and the gifts of the earth.

Hecate

In Greek tradition, Hecate is the goddess of witchcraft, liminal spaces and the crossroads. She is closely tied to Samhain, when the veil is thin, and can be invoked for guidance in ancestral work, divination and banishing.

Autumn tips & recommendations

Ingredient access

Autumn offers an abundance of magical ingredients: apples, pumpkins, squash, acorns, nuts, gourds, corn husks, fallen leaves and seasonal herbs such as sage, rosemary and thyme. If you live in warmer climates, substitute these with whatever local fruits and herbs are plentiful in your region. Collect fallen seeds, nuts or colourful foliage for use in your spells.

Observing nature

This season is rich with symbolism. Watch the falling leaves, which remind us of the beauty of letting go. Notice animals preparing for hibernation or migration, showing us the wisdom of preparation and rest.

Crafting tools

Autumn is the perfect time to gather natural items for magical tools. Acorns and pinecones make excellent talismans for protection. Corn husks can be crafted into dolls for seasonal altars. Fallen leaves can be gathered or pressed for spellwork and offerings.

Best spell types for autumn

Spells for gratitude, shielding, justice, banishing, release and ancestral connection are especially powerful in autumn. It is also a potent time for divination, goal-setting and restorative inner work as you prepare for the winter ahead.

AUTUMN SPELLS

Autumn renewal spell

Just as the trees release their leaves, so too must we release what drains us. This spell is designed to restore your energy and remind you that you are as deserving of care as those you support.

YOU WILL NEED *a cup, a handful of edible wild berries (such as blackberries or blueberries), a pinch of ground cinnamon, a pinch of salt, water and a spoon.*

Find a quiet time when you can sit and reflect on all that you've done this year so far. Congratulate yourself for doing all the mundane life things that everyone else relies on you to do. Fill the cup with a handful of berries you've picked, then add the cinnamon and salt, and a few drops of water. Mash it all together with the back of a spoon to create a paste.

Now think about dropping everyone else's problems and finally reclaiming your own life. You have a unique power, and you were not put on this earth to make life easier for everyone else. Dip your finger into the paste and draw a pentagram (a five-pointed star within a circle, see page 124) on the inside of each forearm. Say the following words:

'By the power of Freyja, I call back my power. I refill my cup. I am as important as anyone else. Enough is enough. So mote it be.'

Sit for a while and remind yourself that you too are important. Wash off the paste when you're ready. You will now begin to do more for yourself.

Autumnal healing spell

This ritual calls on Hygeia, the Greek goddess of health, to send healing and comfort remotely, allowing you to wrap someone in warmth, protection and restorative power, even from afar.

YOU WILL NEED *a photo of the person you wish to heal, a small square of fabric or wool, a white candle, matches and a rose quartz crystal.*

Take the photo of the person you wish to heal and wrap the square of fabric or wool around it as if wrapping them in a blanket. Light the candle and place the wrapped photo in front of it with the rose quartz on top. Say the following words out loud:

'(Name), I send the power and energy of Hygeia to cleanse your body and soul. Day by day, in every way, you become stronger for longer. Day by day, in every way, you gain more strength and stamina. Day by day, in every way, you become you once again, only better and stronger. So mote it be.'

Visualize yourself sending healing energy through the ether in the form of strands of golden thread zooming through the universe to reach the person that needs healing. Allow the candle to safely burn away, then keep the photo and crystal together somewhere safe.

Crystal sanctuary guide

Crystals carry subtle yet powerful vibrations that can harmonize and protect the spaces we live in. By placing certain stones in different rooms, you can create an environment that supports harmony throughout your home.

YOU WILL NEED *crystals.*

Place the crystals in the relevant spaces to realign the energy of each room.

Amethyst – Place in the kitchen for healthy eating or in the bedroom for calming energy.
Aquamarine – Place in your bathroom for rejuvenation.
Black moonstone – Place in your main living room for calm and grounding energy.
Black tourmaline – Place by the front door to keep negativity out.
Carnelian – Place by the front door to welcome abundance.
Citrine – Place in the southeast corner of your home or office to attract financial abundance.
Clear quartz – Place in the most central part of your home for balance and positivity.
Fluorite – Place in your workspace or office to encourage clarity and focus.
Jasper – Keep in the bedroom for grounding energy.
Pink quartz – Place in the bedroom for love and passion.
Pyrite – Place in your workspace or office for prosperity and abundance.
Selenite – Place on a windowsill in your main living room to invite positive energy.
Smoky quartz – Place in your bathroom to balance energy flow.
Turquoise – Place in your dining area to promote conscious eating.
White quartz – Place under your pillow for healthy sleep.

Seasonal refocusing spell

This spell clears confusion and shows you your path, by aligning you with the bright, clarifying light of Theia, goddess of illumination.

YOU WILL NEED *an empty spray bottle, spring water, your favourite essential oil, a pinch of salt, a white tealight candle, matches and a small bell.*

Fill your empty spray bottle with spring water. Add three drops of essential oil and a pinch of salt, and shake well to mix. Next, drip three drops of the essential oil on to the tealight candle, then light the candle and sit in front of it.

Lightly spray yourself with the potion you've made, then ring the bell around your body to clear the energy in the air.

Say the following, while looking into the candle flame:

'I call upon Theia to bring clarity to me. I ask that you remind me of how far I've come and how far I can go. I ask that you release all that is not working for me and bring forth all that will benefit me now. So mote it be.'

Ring the bell around yourself again to bring Theia closer to you. Remain seated and continue staring into the candle until it safely burns away. Finally, ring the bell around your body again. You will feel as though you have been cleansed and will be better able to work out where you want to go next. Keep the spray for future use and shake well every time you spray it. It will last three months.

Autumn altar

Refreshing your altar at the start of autumn clears away the old and welcomes in the new, preparing your magical space for the harvest season ahead. For best results, cast this altar blessing at the beginning of September.

YOU WILL NEED *seasonal flowers, natural twine, a few small pumpkins of different varieties, pinecones, feathers, the Temperance Tarot card, a gold candle, an orange candle, a white candle and matches.*

In the weeks before resetting your altar, pick some of your favourite seasonal flowers and tie them into a bouquet with some natural twine. Hang them upside down somewhere warm to dry out.

Arrange the dried flowers on your altar, along with the pumpkins, pinecones and feathers. Add the Temperance card to your display, for balance and harmony. Arrange the candles on your altar and light all three to signal that your autumn altar is now active. Call upon Persephone to help you through this period of change and renewal. Bless your space by visualizing an orange dome protecting it.

Blow out your candles after a few minutes. Your space is now ready to welcome in the next season. You will notice that your spells are more powerful.

Autumn glow ritual

Autumn is a time of transition, a moment to pause and prepare for the coming months. This spell helps you reset and nurture your body, mind and spirit. For best results, cast this spell on a Sunday evening.

YOU WILL NEED *a couple of acorns, a shower or bath, rose essential oil, lavender essential oil, a pink candle, matches, your favourite face mask and body moisturizer.*

Acorns are associated with growth, so forage for a couple of them in wooded areas. Place them in your bathtub or shower tray. If you're taking a bath, run the bath and add three drops each of lavender and rose oil to the water. Agitate the water before entering the bath to ensure the oils are dispersed. If you're taking a shower, add the drops of oil to the shower tray. As you bathe or shower, say or sing the following words:

'I let go of what is no longer helpful, and welcome in what is good for my heart, body and soul. I deserve all good that comes my way and I banish anything that is not. The new season brings with it new opportunities that will make me grow in a positive way. This is my power. This will be.'

Afterwards, light your candle and apply the face mask. Add three drops each of lavender and rose oil to a handful of body moisturizer and apply it all over your body. Place the acorns on your dressing table to remind you of your growth – and relax for the evening.

Grass & flower seeding ritual

If you're lucky enough to live near the countryside, this is a lovely ritual to connect with nature and yourself. In late summer and early autumn, many grasses and wildflowers have matured seeds, ready to be carried by the wind or animals to new locations.

YOU WILL NEED *a natural area in which to go walking.*

Next time you go for a walk, gently collect a few mature seedheads from grasses or wildflowers (being careful not to take too many from a single plant). As you walk, scatter the seeds behind you, making a wish or setting an intention. Nature will carry your seeds far and wide, and in return, Mother Nature will grant your wish.

Autumn cocoon spell

As autumn unfolds, the world begins to quieten. Just as caterpillars retreat into their cocoons to transform, you can begin to turn inward in order to rest and protect your energy. This spell creates a personal sanctuary, allowing you to step back from the noise of life, restore your spirit and re-emerge when you are ready.

YOU WILL NEED *a walnut in its shell, a knife, a towel (optional), a strand of your own hair, a small crystal of your choice, a small silver charm, glue, a silver candle and matches.*

Carefully prise open the walnut shell without breaking it. If necessary, place it on a towel so that it doesn't roll about. Once the walnut shell is open, discard the walnut.

Place a strand of your hair, a small crystal and a silver charm into one half of the walnut shell, then close it up again. Glue the two halves together, then light the silver candle. Hold the walnut shell in your hands and say the following words:

'I call upon Hecate, goddess of magic and boundaries, to cocoon me and wrap me in your protective bubble so that I have boundaries for peace, self-care and rest. May all my worries be taken away from this day forth, until I am ready to re-enter the world. So mote it be.'

Carry the walnut shell around with you and, when you want to reactivate the cocoon feeling, rub it with your thumb.

Autumn health motivation spell

As the year turns, it's the perfect time to align your intentions with healthier habits, whether through movement, nourishment or simply treating your body with more care. This spell helps you step confidently into a healthier rhythm. For best results, cast during the first two weeks of September.

YOU WILL NEED *a pen, the Ace of Hearts playing card, a white tealight candle, matches and a drawing pin.*

Think about how you want to get healthy and the reason why. Perhaps you want to start running or eating more mindfully, or maybe you want to get fitter by learning to dance or surf.

On the playing card, draw what you want to do to get healthy. For example, you might draw a stick person on a surfboard. Underneath the picture, write an affirmation, such as, 'I can now remain upright on the board and surf small waves.'

Place the card on a flat surface and place the tealight candle on top. Light it and the following words out loud:

'Persephone, goddess of awakening, join me on my new journey. Make it fun and enjoyable, so that I have the power to change. So be it now!'

Allow the candle to safely burn away, then pin the card somewhere where you will see it every day to give you motivation to keep at it. You will more driven to stick with your new regime.

Self-love brew

As the evenings grow darker, take time to reconnect with yourself and nourish your body, heart and mind. This spell acts as a gentle self-love ritual. For best results, cast on a Friday evening.

YOU WILL NEED *240ml (1 cup) milk, a saucepan, 45g (¼ cup) chopped dark or milk chocolate, a pinch of ground cinnamon, a pinch of chilli powder, a wooden spoon, 1 teaspoon rose water, 1 teaspoon orange blossom water and your favourite mug.*

Pour the milk into a saucepan and place over a medium heat to warm through. Once warm, add the chocolate, cinnamon and chilli powder. Stir in a clockwise direction until the chocolate has melted. Allow the mixture to cool a little before adding the rose and orange blossom water. Say the following words:

'With chocolate so sweet, I honour and cherish me. I open my heart to self-love, joy and inner peace. I am worthy, I am radiant, I am complete. So be it.'

Stir your magical hot chocolate drink clockwise again, then pour it into your favourite mug. Sip your drink and, as you do, feel the hot chocolate infusing you with warmth and self-love.

Autumn herb bundle

It's always a good idea to make a new herb bundle as the seasons change. Make this herb bundle anytime during the autumn season.

YOU WILL NEED *a selection of seasonal herbs (such as wild thyme, coriander, fennel, oregano, yarrow, parsley, rosemary, sage and thyme) and natural twine.*

Lay out all your picked herbs on a tray and place them in a sunny area to dry out. Gather the dry herbs into a bundle and tie tightly with the twine, winding it all the way up the pile of herbs.

Your bundle is now ready to use. Light the end, let it smoulder gently, and carry it through your home so that the smoke can cleanse your space.

Remember: after burning your herb bundle, always collect the spent ash, as it will have absorbed the negative energy. Be sure to discard of it away from your home.

First impressions petal charm

A new season brings new opportunities. Perhaps you have an important meeting coming up, or you're meeting someone new for the first time. Whether personal, professional or social, this spell helps you awaken your inner confidence, ensuring you present your best self when it matters most. Perform this charm any time you need to make a good impression.

YOU WILL NEED *petals from your favourite autumn flower and your shoes.*

On the day you wish to make a good first impression, find your favourite autumn flower. Ask the flower to allow you to take a few petals, and pop them into both of your shoes. Empty your shoes of the flower petals the following day.

Swift space cleansing spell

As the natural world begins to slow and retreat, our spaces can accumulate trapped, heavy energy. This spell offers a simple, effective way to reset the atmosphere in your home or workspace.

YOU WILL NEED *a glass of water, salt, vinegar and a spoon.*

Take your glass of water and add three pinches of salt and a good squirt of vinegar. Mix the solution in an anticlockwise direction to activate the energy-cleanse spell. Leave the full glass anywhere in your home or office overnight. You will feel a change in atmosphere the following morning.

Autumn Book of Shadows

A Book of Shadows is a personal magical journal where a witch records spells, rituals, correspondences and magical observations. It serves as both a guide to and a reflection of your unique practice, evolving over time as your knowledge and connection with the natural world grows.

YOU WILL NEED *your Book of Shadows, foraged items and writing or drawing supplies.*

During your autumn walks, collect fallen leaves, nuts, seeds, flowers and other natural treasures. Take them home and document your findings in your Book of Shadows, making a note of their magical properties for future spells and rituals. Over time, your book will become a living record of both nature's bounty and your personal practice.

Nature's triangle grounding ritual

In our fast-paced modern world, it is essential to ground yourself and reconnect with the natural rhythms around you. The simplest way to do this is to take a mindful walk in a field, forest or any natural space, and gather some items that call to you.

YOU WILL NEED *a basket or cloth bag.*

As you walk, notice the first three natural items that draw your attention. Perhaps you'll see a pebble, a pinecone, a fallen leaf or a conker. Gather them in your basket or bag. Bring your treasures home and place them on a windowsill in the shape of a triangle. Sit quietly for a few moments, focusing on the energy of each item and allowing yourself to feel the connection between the earth and your body. As you breathe deeply, remind yourself of the beauty of nature, and let that grounding energy settle within you.

Step into your intentions spell

Magic doesn't always require elaborate rituals, rare ingredients or specific lunar phases. Often, the simplest spells are the most effective, because the strength lies in your intention. This spell is perfect for busy days when you need to ensure your goals progress smoothly.

YOU WILL NEED *a small piece of paper, a pen and your shoes.*

On a small piece of paper, write down what you want to happen today. Fold the paper three times and pop it into your shoe. You will literally be setting the spell in motion every time you walk.

Oak-leaf fire healing spell

As autumn settles in, the season's energy lends itself to restorative and cleansing magic. Oak leaves, long associated with strength and protection in Greek, Norse and Celtic folklore, can be used to help ward off illness and support recovery for yourself or another household member.

YOU WILL NEED *as many fallen oak leaves as you can find and an open fire or a dish or cauldron, a silver candle and matches.*

Gather as many oak leaves as you can find and dry them on a sunny windowsill or in a warm room until they are crisp. If you have an open fire, carefully throw the dried leaves into the flames and say:

'Sickness be gone. Wellness return. By the power of these leaves I do burn.'

If you do not have a fireplace, place the dried leaves in a bowl or cauldron and light a white or silver candle next to it. Visualize the candle's flame drawing the illness or discomfort away from the person, then carefully allow the candle to safely burn down while continuing to focus on sending healing energy.

The unwell person should begin to feel better within 24 hours.

Persephone's autumn transition spell

In Greek mythology, Persephone (see page 149) descends into the Underworld each autumn, mirroring the turning of the seasons - a time when nature retreats inward. This spell welcomes her gentle guidance as you transition into the calm, grounding energy of autumn.

YOU WILL NEED *a thin white candle, a heatproof plate, one pomegranate, a knife, matches and an outdoor space.*

Secure the candle on a heatproof plate. Deseed the pomegranate and set it on the plate, next to the candle. Take it outside on a still day, light the candle, and say the following words:

'Persephone, I give you this offering as my thanks for protecting nature and our seasons. May you take this as a gift in exchange for a peaceful autumn within the world. So mote it be.'

Let the candle burn down safely. Once extinguished, remove the candle and any residual wax from the plate and leave the pomegranate outside as an offering for nature, along with the pomegranate seeds.

Pumpkin seed cleansing ritual

Our homes often carry energy from the people who frequent them or the objects we bring inside. Lingering trapped energy can feel heavy or misaligned with your own vibrations. This simple yet powerful spell will purify your space.

YOU WILL NEED *a bowl, salt, a handful of dry pumpkin seeds and a bell.*

Half-fill the bowl with salt, then place the pumpkin seeds on top. Take the bowl into a room in your house and place it on the floor in the middle of the room. Say the following words as you ring the bell over the bowl:

'Negative energy, you must now leave. I no longer allow you to be in my home or about my person. Negative energy, you must now leave. I exile you and bring in only good and positive energy from here forth. This is my power.'

Repeat this procedure in every room in your home. Every time you buy something, even if it's new, it can still hold another person's energy. When you bring a new item into your home, ring a bell over it and say the banishing words above.

Seasonal cheer brew

While plants and animals slow down at this time of year and prepare for rest, we often continue our busy routines, leaving little space for emotional recalibration. This spell lifts your spirits and restores emotional balance using comforting herbal magic and the power of Modron, goddess of harvest, abundance and healing.

YOU WILL NEED *a few peppermint leaves, a few lemon balm leaves, a knife, a jug, dried ginger, hot water, a strainer and your favourite mug or cup.*

Clean and roughly chop the peppermint and lemon balm to release their natural oils, then add to jug. Add a few pinches of dried ginger and mix the ingredients with your hands, saying:

'Modron, keeper of the cauldron, I call to you to help lift me now. May you lighten my load and pave the way to brighter days. So mote it be.'

Add enough hot water to cover all the ingredients and leave to steep for ten minutes. Strain the liquid through a strainer into your favourite mug or cup. Drink your mood-boosting cuppa, knowing that everything is going to be OK.

Fallen leaf confidence garland

This ritual harnesses the natural power of fallen leaves to boost your self-assurance. It also calls upon Flaunta, the Roman goddess of confidence. For best results, cast this spell on a Sunday evening.

YOU WILL NEED *10 fallen leaves, a green candle and matches, a green pen, a hole punch and natural twine.*

Try to gather leaves that are of a similar size. Light your green candle, then on each leaf write one letter of the word 'CONFIDENCE'. Punch a hole in the top of each leaf. Thread your twine through the holes, tying a knot between each leaf, until you have a banner of leaves that spell out 'CONFIDENCE'. Hang your banner somewhere you will see it for the next 24 hours. As you hang it, say:

'I call upon the goddess Flaunta to bring me confidence, so that I may feel worthy of being me once again. So mote it be.'

Allow the candle to burn away safely. Leave your banner up for the next 24 hours, then dismantle it and return the leaves to nature to decompose.

Autumnal threshold cleanse

Cleansing the entrance to your home (or room) allows the energy of the new season to flow freely while washing out the old. For best results, cast this spell at the start of the new season.

YOU WILL NEED *a bucket of warm water, peppermint essential oil, rosemary essential oil, a few sage leaves, clove essential oil, orange essential oil, a cloth and salt.*

To the bucket of warm water, add six drops each of peppermint oil and rosemary oil (to welcome positive energy), a few sage leaves and six drops of clove oil (to protect against negative energy), and six drops of orange oil (to welcome abundance and prosperity). Take a cloth and wash your front door with this potion. Spread a line of salt across the threshold. After the cleanse, leave the potion to dry naturally on the door.

Quick fortune spell

Autumn is the perfect time to invite good fortune into your life. This simple spell attracts wealth quickly.

YOU WILL NEED *dried cinnamon, a green candle, matches and a gold coin.*

Sprinkle a pinch of cinnamon around the green candle in a clockwise direction, then light the candle. Hold the coin in your palms and say:

'Luck, prosperity and light, good fortune come to me this night.'

Allow the candle to safely burn away, then dust the coin with cinnamon and keep it in your purse.

Autumn broom

As the Wheel of the Year turns toward Mabon, it's the perfect time to refresh your witch's broom, inviting the energy of the season into your magical practice. This broom will embody autumn's protection, wisdom and grounding.

YOU WILL NEED *a broom (see page 24 if you want to make one), sprigs of rosemary, thyme and sage, orange and black ribbon, a glue gun and glue, and items of personal jewellery (optional).*

Take your broom and tie the herb sprigs into the brush section for protection and seasonal energy. Wind the orange and black ribbons around the broom handle, securing them with glue. Add any personal charms or jewellery you wish to make the broom uniquely yours.

To consecrate your broom and call upon the autumn goddess, stand before it and say:

'Modron, guardian of the harvest and the turning wheel, bless this broom with your strength, protection and wisdom. May it sweep away what no longer serves me and carry the blessings of autumn in every motion. So mote it be.'

Place the broom on the ground and jump over it three times to activate its magic.

Mabon harvest gratitude jar

This spell focuses on harvesting and honouring the bounty around you, fostering connection with nature's cycles. Perform this harvest blessing on or around Mabon.

YOU WILL NEED *a basket and a jar with a lid.*

Before you begin gathering, take a quiet moment outdoors. Close your eyes and breathe deeply, attuning yourself to the energy of the earth and the changing season. Say:

'Modron, I honour your gifts. May I take only what I need, with gratitude and care.'

Take a walk through a natural area, collecting seasonal goodies like hazelnuts, chestnuts, acorns or berries. Visualize each nut or fruit glowing with golden light, storing energy and prosperity for the months ahead. Place the items gently in your basket, imagining them filling not just your basket but also your life with abundance. Remember that many animals rely on these foods to survive the winter, so please only take what you need.

Once home, dry your harvest in a warm, airy place or near a sunny window. Once dry, transfer the items to a jar and whisper:

'Preserved by earth and sun, may these gifts sustain and protect, bringing nourishment and fortune as the seasons turn.'

Keep your jar in a dark space until the spring.

★ Oak tree manifestation spell

Oak trees symbolize strength and endurance. Folklore says that when you plant an acorn and make a wish, that wish will grow as the acorn grows. This spell uses a fallen acorn as a vessel for your manifestations, and is perfect for fixing your sights on long-term goals that may take many years to achieve.

YOU WILL NEED *an acorn, a jug of water, a small plant and compost.*

To check if your acorn is suitable for planting, pop it into a jug of water. If it sinks, it's good to use. If it floats, it won't grow and you'll need to find another.

Fill your plant pot two-thirds full of compost, then add the acorn. Cover it with more compost. As you do this, visualize the long-term goal you are aiming for. This could be getting married or buying your first house. Believe that, as your acorn grows, you will be growing towards your goal. Water your seedling well and keep it in a sunny area.

As the seedling grows, you will have to carefully transfer it into a bigger pot. When it's about 15cm (6in) tall, you can plant it out in your garden, a woodland or a field. As the years pass and your acorn grows into an oak tree, your dream will be coming true.

Mabon healing broth

As the Autumn Equinox (Mabon) arrives, the season of harvest reminds us to give thanks for the abundance this time of year has to offer. This magical broth uses the seasonal bounty to nourish both body and spirit, along with cinnamon and bay leaves for love, peace and health.

YOU WILL NEED *a selection of seasonal vegetables (such as pumpkin, parsnips, turnips, carrots, swede and potatoes), a large stockpot or cauldron, boiling water, a pinch each of salt and sugar, a vegetable stock cube, 3 bay leaves, 1 cinnamon stick, lentils or other pulses and a wooden spoon.*

Traditionally, a witch's broth would consist of any produce they could find, and they would literally throw it in the pot. And this is what you should do too. Chop your chosen vegetables and add them to the pot or cauldron. Pour over enough boiling water to cover the produce, then add the salt, sugar, stock cube, bay leaves, cinnamon stick and lentils or pulses. Place over a low heat and leave to cook for at least 6 hours, stirring occasionally.

Remove the bay leaves and cinnamon, and ladle the broth into bowls. Eat with the intention that all will be well in life for you - and it will be.

Mabon space renewal

As day and night stand equal, Mabon is the perfect moment to cleanse both yourself and your sacred space to rebalance the energies, inviting harmony and ensuring the potency of your future spells.

YOU WILL NEED *your altar and its contents, an empty spray bottle, lemon juice, lavender essential oil, spring water, your favourite music and a natural cleaning cloth.*

Clear your altar of all your tools and set them aside. Fill the spray bottle with a few drops of lemon juice, 13 drops of lavender oil and spring water. Give it a good shake. Play your favourite music in the background to make the task more fun.

Spray the surface area where you practise your magic and leave it for a few minutes before wiping it down. Now spray every non-porous item that you use in your spells and rituals, including candles, holders, ornaments, etc. Allow the potion to linger for a few minutes before wiping clean.

Before putting the items back in place, spray your potion into the air and walk through the spray. Say out loud:

'Modron, please bless me and bless this sacred space. So mote it be'.'

Put back all your altar items, but make sure you get rid of any used items, such as half-spent candles, herb dust or scraps of paper.

Equinox sunset spell

Autumn sunsets carry a quiet kind of magic. This spell harnesses the transformative energy of the Autumn Equinox to set intentions for the season ahead. For best results, cast this spell at sunset on Mabon.

YOU WILL NEED *a blanket, your journal, a pen, a separate piece of paper and a trowel.*

Half an hour before the sun begins to set, go to your favourite outside spot and spread a blanket on the ground to sit on. Take out your journal and, on a clean page, write down your intentions for the next quarter of the year. Only write things that excite you, and imagine how you will be feeling once they have manifested. The key here is 'feel'. Your goals and dreams will manifest very quickly if you can summon up the feeling or having them, rather than just thinking about what you want.

When you're happy with what you've written, write key bullet points summarising your goals on the separate piece of paper. Roll the paper into a scroll and, just as the sun sets, dig a hole in the ground, place the scroll in the hole and bury it. Wait until the sun fully sets. Your intentions will soon become reality.

Ego release jar spell

Even the most grounded of witches can sometimes find their ego running the show. This spell is designed to help you release ego-driven frustrations. For best results, cast during a full-moon phase.

YOU WILL NEED *small pieces of paper, a black pen, a jar with a lid, ground black pepper and ash from an incense stick.*

Sit and write down anything that upsets or angers you in your life. This could be something your mother said that has stuck with you since your childhood, or it could be that your boss passed you up for promotion. Whatever it is, it's your ego telling you that life sucks - and every good witch knows that this kind of energy is no good for you. When you're done, pop each piece of paper into the jar and say:

'That's it, no more will I give my energy to this. So mote it be.'

Sprinkle some black pepper into the jar, along with some ash from an incense stick to signal that you are done with being the victim of your ego. Place the jar in a dark cupboard and keep adding to it every time you remember something that annoyed, upset or hurt you.

Wait for a month, then burn the papers and start again. This process will help you to free your mind and energy every month.

★ Corn offering gratitude spell

In Celtic folklore, corn symbolizes fertility, abundance and the cycles of life. It is often offered to deities like Modron, the mother goddess of the harvest, to give thanks for the season's bounty. For best results, cast this spell on Mabon.

YOU WILL NEED *a white tealight candle, matches and a fresh corn on the cob.*

On the evening of Mabon, light the tealight candle and hold the corn in your hands. Repeat the following words three times:

'Modron, I offer you this corn as my way of thanks. May you continue to protect and support me in all that I do. So mote it be.'

Allow the candle to safely burn away, then take the corn outside and leave it somewhere for the birds to find. When all the corn has gone, you can be assured that Modron has received your message.

Harvest Moon creativity elixir

The Harvest Moon is the full moon closest to the autumnal equinox, and it usually occurs in September or early October. It carries powerful energy for creativity, insight and inspiration. This spell harnesses that energy to reignite your mind. For best results, cast on the night of the Harvest Moon.

YOU WILL NEED *a silver spoon and a cup of tea, coffee or hot chocolate.*

Take the silver spoon outside under the full Harvest Moon. Hold it up so that the moonlight reflects off its surface and on to you. Stay like this, absorbing the moon's energy, for three minutes. As you do so, focus on your intention: clarity, inspiration or creativity in a specific project or study.

Return indoors and prepare a cup of coffee, tea or hot chocolate. Stir the drink with your silver spoon three times clockwise, visualizing your ideas flowing freely and any mental blocks dissolving. Sip slowly, imagining the moon's energy infusing your mind with creativity.

★ Harvest Moon manifestation spell

The Harvest Moon (see above) carries an energy of clarity and forward momentum. This spell uses moon water to capture this moon's energy and channel it into your manifestations. For best results, cast on the night of the Harvest Moon.

YOU WILL NEED *a silver safety pin, a piece of edible rice paper, a glass of water and a saucer.*

Think about what you want to manifest for this season. Use the silver safety pin to scratch a word or symbol relating to your wish into the edible paper.

When you've finished, place a glass of water outside under the full moon, with a saucer on top to cover it. Leave overnight.

The following morning, retrieve your moon water. Eat the edible paper, then drink the moon water. Pin the safety pin into an item of clothing you wear regularly. You will see your wishes quickly manifesting during the next season.

Harvest Moon wish spell

Traditionally, the Harvest Moon (see page 164) signals a time to reap the rewards of your efforts and set intentions for the coming months. This spells allows you to work with its energy to accelerate your goals. For best results, cast this spell outside or in a well-ventilated space on the morning of the Harvest Moon, or on a Monday.

YOU WILL NEED *a small piece of paper, a pen, dried mugwort, dried rosemary, dried marigold flowers (or autumnal flowers of your choice), a pestle and mortar, a small cloth bag, a cauldron or fireproof dish and matches.*

Think about what it is you would like to come into your life quite quickly. Write it down on the piece of paper, then fold it up as small as you can make it and set it aside. Combine the mugwort, rosemary and marigold and grind to a fine dust using a pestle and mortar. Tip the ground ingredients into the cloth bag and add the small piece of paper.

Place the bag in your cauldron or fireproof dish and set fire to it. As you do, say the following words:

'On this Moon's Day, I call you to grant my power to accelerate all my desires contained in this bag. I ask that you take this into the air with you and allow it to travel throughout the universe for my wish to be granted. This will be so.'

Wait until the bag has safely burned away. Once the ashes are cool, sprinkle them across the threshold of your home. Look out for magical synchronicities and coincidences – these signal the success of your spell.

Harvest Moon mood shield

The Harvest Moon (see page 164) brings a powerful energy of abundance and protection. Use its bright golden light to shield your mood and personal energy from negativity and protect your peace. For best results, cast this spell on the night of the Harvest Moon.

YOU WILL NEED *a bottle of spring water, salt and a piece of jewellery.*

When the moon is full, go outside into your garden and draw a large circle (big enough for you to sit in) on the ground with the spring water. Inside the water circle, draw a smaller circle with the salt. Sit in the middle of the circles and hold the piece of jewellery in both hands. Look up to the moon and say the following words:

'Mother Moon, Mother Moon, I call on your protection to preserve my energy and prevent negativity from seeping in. I ask that you protect my energy at all costs and stop any bad vibes from entering my soul. This is my request; so mote it be.'

Stand up and turn clockwise in the circle three times, then jump out of the circle. The following morning, sweep away the circle. Wear your item of jewellery as often as you can to keep others' moods from affecting you.

Seven days of gratitude spell

Gratitude is one of the most powerful forms of magic, raising your energetic frequency and drawing more blessings into your life. Cast this spell over seven consecutive days.

YOU WILL NEED ***a white tealight candle, matches, a 3-minute timer, a notebook and a pen.***

Find a quiet moment when you can pause for at least three minutes to just be. Light the white tealight candle and set the three-minute timer. In your notebook, write: 'Things to be grateful for #1'. Now think about everything you currently have that you are blessed with, big or small. There are so many little things that we often take for granted. Keep writing until the three minutes are up. Read your list and silently thank the gods and goddesses for providing you with all that you have. Blow out the candle and keep it for the following day.

Repeat the procedure for the next six days. By day seven, you will begin to notice more good things coming that you can add to your list.

Harvest career spell

This is the perfect time of year to seek advancement in your life, especially in your career. This spell uses crystal energy to open the way for new job opportunities. For best results, cast this spell on the Thursday closest to Mabon.

YOU WILL NEED ***a yellow candle, matches, a small citrine crystal or tiger's eye crystal, paper, a pen, a wire crystal cage and a silver chain.***

Light the yellow candle and place the citrine or tiger's eye crystal in front of it. Look into the flame of the candle and think about the benefits of receiving the promotion or career development you are hoping for. This could be things like more money or greater influence. Write these perks on your piece of paper. Now, visualize in detail how this career advancement would unfold – perhaps you are called into your boss's office, or a major brand reaches out to work with your business.

Drop three drops of the candle wax on to the paper, then let the candle safely burn away. Keep the paper somewhere safe – perhaps in the same place where you keep your current work contract.

Take the small crystal and place it in the wire crystal case, then thread the silver chain through it. Wear it as a necklace every day when you go into work until you get your promotion.

Lucky 13th prosperity spell

Non-witches believe that Friday 13th is unlucky. However, for witches it is one of the luckiest days of the year. Every year will have at least one Friday 13th, but there can be up to three, and it is considered to be a magical day to cast spells. This spell is designed to bring money and prosperity to the spellcaster. Perform it on a Friday 13th.

YOU WILL NEED *a small piece of paper, a black pen, a green pen and a potted plant (ideally a money plant).*

Draw 13 cats on the paper and colour them in using the black pen. With the green marker pen, outline each cat. Say the following words:

'Thirteen cats, all of them black,
thirteen cats, all of them green.
Prosperity cometh to me.
On this lucky day, that is so feared,
the gods will look down upon me, my wish adhered.'

Roll the piece of paper into a scroll and bury it in the earth in your plant pot, being careful not to disturb the plant's roots too much. As the paper dissolves into the soil, money will come into your life.

Autumn Equinox drink spell

By crafting a simple harvest drink of seasonal fruits and nuts, you can ingest Mabon's energies of vitality and prosperity. For best results, cast this spell on or around Mabon.

YOU WILL NEED *seasonal berries (such as blackberries or blueberries), seasonal nuts (such as sweet chestnuts, beech nuts or hazelnuts), a blender, water, ice cubes, salt and a cup.*

Put a handful or two of the berries and nuts into a blender. Add 300ml (10fl oz) water, a couple of ice cubes and a pinch of salt. The salt is not just a magical ingredient; it will also bring out the flavour of the berries.

Place the lid on the blender and blend the ingredients together until it looks like a smoothie. Pour the mixture into a cup and, before you drink it, say the following words:

'Mother Nature, I give my thanks. On this Mabon I harvest your plentiful bounty, to welcome in the new season with blessings, peace and love. May the following season bring me all three. So mote it be.'

Drink the smoothie slowly and with intention to invite the new season into your life.

Ribbon magic three ways

★ Part one:
Knots of intention ribbon spell

Ribbon magic is a modern adaptation of the ancient craft of knot magic, a technique used to transform intentions into reality. Tying a knot in a ribbon focuses your energy and strengthens your intention. This spell calls for *Leven*, an old Celtic word meaning strength.

YOU WILL NEED *a length of ribbon in a colour associated with your desire (see page 93 for colour correspondences).*

Sit quietly with your ribbon and begin tying nine knots in it, spaced evenly apart. As you do so, say the following words:

'By knot of one, the spell has begun.
By knot of two, I ask of you.
By knot of three, to bring to me.
By knot of four, all that I adore.
By knot of five, I feel alive.
By knot of six, you shall fix.
By knot of seven, I call for Leven.
By knot of eight, this is my fate.
By knot of nine, this will be mine.
So mote it be.'

Traditionally, the caster would tie the ribbon in their hair until their wish was manifested. If you don't wish to do this, you can just put it in a safe place.

★ Part two:
Tree of wishes ribbon spell

This ribbon spell invites you to work with the transitional autumnal energies, tying your wishes to the branches so the wind can release them into the universe.

YOU WILL NEED *ribbon in the appropriate colour for your wish (see page 93), a pen and a tree with bare branches.*

Take your chosen ribbon and write your wish on it, then gently tie it to a branch on the tree. If you are hoping for a combination of different desires, you can choose more than one ribbon, and either hang each strand separately or plait them together as one.

Part three:
Moonlit ribbon protection charm

Silver and white are traditionally linked to the moon and its protective energies, so ribbons in these colours can be infused with moonlight to create protective charms. For best results, create this charm on the night of a full moon.

YOU WILL NEED *silver or white ribbon and a tree with bare branches.*

Gently tie the ribbon to the tree, then leave overnight under the full moon. The next day, the ribbon can be tied to your bag, belt loop or jacket zipper to provide ongoing protection.

Autumnal heart spell

As the days grow shorter and the nights cooler, autumn invites cozy companions to share in her warmth and slowness. This spell helps attract love or deep companionship into your life. For best results, cast on a Friday evening.

YOU WILL NEED *a pink candle, matches, pink paper, a heart-shaped paper cutter and 3 small pinecones.*

Light the candle and place it in front of you. While it burns, cut out 36 paper hearts from the pink paper. Visualize what sort of person you would like to spend the autumnal months cozied up to as you push 12 paper hearts between the scales of each pinecone. Now arrange the pinecones around the candle and say:

'By the power of three, I ask of thee,
to bring to me a romance that I will see.
A person who is my match, someone who is my ideal catch.
By the power of three, I command thee.
One, two, three.'

Allow the candle to burn safely away, then place the three pinecones in different rooms in your home. Within a few weeks, you will meet someone to share the new season with.

Autumn wisdom spell

As the season shifts into autumn, the natural world focuses on preparation and gathering strength for winter. This spell is ideal for anyone seeking to build on that energy by embarking on a new learning journey, whether that involves starting a course, picking up a new hobby or exploring an area of personal study. Cast this spell three days before you intend to begin.

YOU WILL NEED *a large horse chestnut leaf, a black pen, a white candle and matches.*

Try to find a large leaf that has fallen from the tree, rather than picking a fresh one. Lay the leaf on a flat surface. On each segment of the leaf, write down what you hope your new learning experience will bring you - this might be improved confidence, new skills or a way to meet new friends.

When you're happy with what you've written, place the leaf underneath the candle and light the candle. Say the following words:

'By the power of Hecate, bring to me all that I need to make this next chapter a good one. May I progress to greater heights and have no worries at all. So mote it be.'

Allow the candle to safely burn down, then return the leaf to the tree where you found it.

★ Garden wishing-well spell

This spell invites you outside just before the weather turns to create a dedicated space in your garden from where you can send out your desires into the universe, helping them take root and grow. For best results, begin during a full-moon phase.

YOU WILL NEED *a spade, a large flowerpot with drainage holes, chicken wire, wire-cutters, some fallen leaves and a pen.*

Find a secluded area in your garden that no one will walk over. Dig a hole in the ground big enough to hold your flowerpot, then place the pot in the hole so that it is sunken into the ground. Cut a circle of chicken wire large enough to fit over the top of the flowerpot. This will keep any small creatures from falling in.

Take a leaf and write on it one wish. It's advisable to write just one wish per day, otherwise the universe might get things muddled up. Close your eyes and scrunch up the leaf, then drop it into your wishing well.

You can decorate the surroundings of your wishing well if you want to by planting flowers and herbs, or arranging crystals around it. Use your wishing well anytime you want to make a quick wish.

★ Blessings on the wind spell

This spell uses the crisp autumn breeze to carry your intentions of joy and blessings to others.

YOU WILL NEED *a bunch of dried fallen leaves, a hole-punch and a tote bag.*

Go for a walk and pick up as many fallen leaves as you can, in as many different colours as possible. Return home and spread out your collection of leaves on a table. Spend some time with a hole-punch making holes in the leaves, then empty the hole-punch confetti into the tote bag. Head out with your bag, scattering handfuls of your leaf confetti on the doorsteps of your friends' or neighbours' homes and random houses, on cars, on pavements, outside public buildings – anywhere you feel needs a sprinkle of happiness. As you sprinkle your blessings, say the following words:

'I bless you with happiness, joy and love on this otherwise ordinary day of ours.'

Your autumn blessings will bring joy to whomever you choose, and yet they will be unaware of why their luck has changed. This act also raises your own vibrational frequency, bringing more blessings your way – win, win.

'Yes or no' dice divination spell

Dice have long been used as fortune-telling tools. Ancient artifacts have shown that Egyptians used animal bones as dice in their divination. This quick spell uses a single die to provide yes-or-no guidance, helping you make choices with clarity.

YOU WILL NEED *a six-sided die.*

Simply ask a yes-or-no question out loud or in your head, then roll the die. Odd numbers mean no and even numbers mean yes. Don't keep asking the same question to get another result!

★ Fireplace wish spell

As the nights lengthen and the weather grows cooler, we are drawn towards cozy rituals. Use the warm, transformative energy of your hearth or an outdoor firepit this season to send your wishes into the universe. For best results, perform this spell on a Saturday evening.

YOU WILL NEED *an open fire or outside firepit, a pinecone and a marker pen.*

Sit by the fire or firepit and write your wish on the underside of the pinecone. Close your eyes and toss the pinecone into the flames. Your wish will soon come true.

★ Apple divination spell

Nature offers us many ways to gain insight and guidance. This spell helps you connect with your intuition and divine answers for the months ahead.

YOU WILL NEED *an apple and a small knife.*

Think about the question you want answered or the guidance you seek. Carefully cut the apple in half horizontally to reveal the core, which resembles a five-pointed star - much like a pentagram. Look closely at the seeds inside the apple. If the seeds are all whole, the answer is yes or that you are on the right path. If the seeds are cut in half or some are missing, the answer is no or that there will be challenges ahead.

Palm key protection charm

As the nights grow longer and the days cooler, it's easy to feel a little more vulnerable when moving through the world. This quick protection spell draws on the symbolic power of a key to ward off unwanted energy.

YOU WILL NEED *a pen.*

Using the pen, draw a key on the palm of your non-dominant hand, then press both hands together to unlock the power. You are now protected.

New-moon portal spell

Autumn is a season of change, when nature readies itself for the quiet months ahead. This spell harnesses that energy, using the new moon to open a portal through which your new intentions and desires can flow. Cast this spell in a well-ventilated space during a new-moon phase.

YOU WILL NEED *a yellow candle, matches, 3 bay leaves, a citrine crystal, a clear quartz crystal, a fluorite crystal, paper, a pen and a cauldron or fireproof dish.*

Light your candle and say:

'The spell has begun; the intentions I make today will be on their way.'

Place the three bay leaves around the candle and put one crystal on each leaf. Sit and think about your life at the moment, then write down nine things for which you are currently grateful.

Draw a line underneath, then write down nine things that you would like to manifest in your life. This could be anything from material possessions to world peace. Place your non-dominant hand over the paper and draw around the outside of it.

Light the right-hand corner of the paper using the candle flame, then drop it into the cauldron or fireproof dish. Say:

'I send my thanks and my requests into the portal today. May it accept my gratitude and accept my intentions. So be it.'

Light the three bay leaves and drop them into the cauldron or fireproof dish. When the bay leaves and paper have safely burned away, blow out the candle and put your crystals back on your altar. The universe's portal will do the rest.

Evil eye protection spell

As autumn deepens and the veil between worlds thins, it becomes necessary to protect yourself from negative energies. This spell channels ancient wisdom to shield you from harmful intentions, reflecting them back to the sender. For best results, cast this spell on a Saturday.

YOU WILL NEED *a black pen and a large leaf (larger than your hand).*

Place your non-dominant hand on the leaf and use the black pen to draw around it. Now draw an open eye in the centre of the shape. Say:

'May every evil eye in my life go blind.'

Scrunch up the leaf and scatter the pieces outside.

Energetic home reset spell

Just as fallen leaves make way for fresh growth, decluttering and cleansing your home removes stagnant energy that can cloud both your mind and your magic.

YOU WILL NEED *a basket or bag and cleaning supplies.*

Move through your home holding the basket or bag, and gather anything that no longer serves you – objects or clutter that feel energetically 'heavy'. Set them aside and take them to a charity shop as soon as possible. Now clean your space. Before you begin cleaning each room, stand in the doorway and clap your hands firmly in every corner. The sharp sound breaks up stagnant energy in the room.

Career-change charm

Autumn reminds us that it's OK to embrace change. This spell calls on Modron (see page 149) to help you focus your energy on obtaining a new job or changing careers. For best results, cast on a Sunday.

YOU WILL NEED *the Fool Tarot card, something relating to your desired career (such as a pen if you want to be a novelist, or a bottle of nail polish if you want to open a nail salon), a green candle, a blue candle, an orange candle and matches.*

The Fool Tarot card represents new beginnings. Place it on top of or next to the item relating to your desired career. Light all three candles in any order. Green is for prosperity, blue is for success and orange is for creativity. Say the following words:

'Modron, bring me luck, power and tenacity to begin my new career as (name it). Give me the strength to see this change through with ease. May I be successful in my chosen field. So be it now.'

Clap your hands three times over the Fool card and allow the candles to burn safely away. Return the Fool card to the deck and wait for your intention to be realized.

Pumpkin prosperity spell

Autumn is the time for pumpkins. As well as being associated with the celebration of Halloween, their seeds are said to bring prosperity. For best results, cast this spell on or around Samhain.

YOU WILL NEED *a pumpkin, a knife, a paper towel and salt and pepper.*

When you carve your pumpkin and scoop out its insides, pick the seeds from the pulp and clean them. Lay them out on a paper towel in a warm space for several days to dry. Once dry, sprinkle them with a little salt and pepper, then choose nine seeds and eat them one by one, visualizing the prosperity they will bring you.

Samhain spirit shield spell

At Samhain, the veil between the worlds is at its thinnest. With so much spiritual energy flowing freely, not every presence that crosses over is welcome. This spell will protect you from unwanted energies while keeping you open to positive ancestral connections. Cast it once on the morning of Samhain, and again when you finish your witchcraft in the evening.

YOU WILL NEED *a white candle, a white quartz crystal and matches.*

On the morning of Samhain, set your candle in a safe place where it won't be disturbed. Wash your white quartz under a tap to clear any negative energy from it, then place it in front of the candle. Light the candle and meditate on the flame for a few minutes, then say the following words out loud:

'In this moment, I call upon only positive energy to enter my world. From people to places, to realms and dimensions, I stand firm in my safety, sovereignty and peace. So mote it be.'

Allow the candle to safely burn down halfway then blow it out.

When you have finished casting spells, practising divination or contacting your ancestors, relight the candle once more and say the following words:

'I thank you for your connection to the spirit realm. I now close the door to any and all negative energy that may have come by to say hello. I send you back with love and light so that you may go on your way this magical night. So mote it be.'

Allow the candle to safely burn away fully, then place the crystal in the room where you cast any spells this Samhain.

Ancestral connection two ways

Part one:
Ancestral spirit spell

During Samhain, the barrier between our world and the realm of ancestors is at its most permeable. Cast this spell before midnight on Halloween to open a sacred channel of communication.

YOU WILL NEED *a white candle, matches, a crystal ball or a bowl of water and a pashmina or large throw.*

Prepare a space where you will not be disturbed for an hour or so. Light your candle and place it in front of you. Say the following inviting prayer:

'I call upon Hecate to bring forth my dearly departed ancestors and friends from other realms. I only allow positive energy in to connect to me. My spirit guides will block all other energy from connecting with me.'

You have opened the portal to the spirit world. Stare into the candle flame and mentally ask for your ancestors to talk to you. The flame might flicker or grow. This means that you have made a connection.

Place your crystal ball or bowl of water in front of you, then cover both your head and the ball or water with the pashmina or throw. Gaze into the crystal ball or water. You may see images, faces or words relating to your loved ones.

When you've finished, close the connection by saying:

'I thank you for coming forth. I now close this connection and bid you a safe farewell. So mote it be.'

Part two:
Thin veil divination

Samhain is the ideal time to connect with your ancestors to ask for guidance from your spirit guides. Perform this scrying spell before midnight on Samhain.

YOU WILL NEED *a bowl, spring water, a purple or blue candle, matches, salt, your phone and a large black cloth.*

Fill a bowl with spring water and light the candle. Draw a circle of salt around where you are sitting – make sure you include the bowl and candle in the circle. This is to protect you while you scry. Ask out loud for only your ancestors or guardian spirits to step forward.

Set your phone to record, then place the cloth over your head and the bowl. Close your eyes, take a few deep breaths and mentally ask if anyone is there. Open your eyes and look into the water.

You may hear or see words in your mind or in the water. Say whatever you hear or see out loud so that your phone can pick it up. Keep asking if anyone has any words of wisdom for you. When you are happy to leave the spirit world, say the following:

'Thank you for connecting today. I now close this session safely, so that you may return to where you belong.'

Blow out the candle and clear away the bowl of water and the salt circle. Wait for ten minutes to adjust back to our world, then listen to your recording.

Halloween release ritual

At Halloween, people would traditionally light fires, carve gourds and perform rituals to protect their homes and themselves from harmful influences. This spell channels that protective energy to banish negativity from your life. Begin this ritual seven days before Halloween.

YOU WILL NEED *2 small pumpkins, a knife, a spoon, a black pen, ground black pepper, salt, chilli powder, 14 black tealight candles and matches.*

Seven days before Halloween, carve out the insides of the two pumpkins. On the side of one pumpkin, write your own name. On the side of the other, write the person or problem you wish to remove from your life. Place a pinch of pepper, salt and chilli powder into each pumpkin, then place them on a table where they won't be disturbed.

Put a black tealight candle into each pumpkin and light them while saying the following words:

'Exterminare, Exterminare,
(Name of person/problem), you should now beware.
The spell has begun and now you're done.
Within seven days, you will be on your way.
I no longer care, Exterminare.'

Allow the candles to safely burn away. The next day, replace them with new ones and repeat the ritual. Do this at the same time every day for seven days. After the seventh day, throw the pumpkins away.

Samhain dream spell

Samhain is the season of endings and beginnings. This spell honours that balance by offering food to nature in exchange for a wish granted. Cast this spell on or around Samhain.

YOU WILL NEED *a paper bag, a gold pen, a handful of birdseed or nuts, natural twine, scissors and a tree.*

Sit quietly for half an hour and think of all the things that you would like to manifest in your life. They could be emotional, physical or material things, or a combination of all three. Write them on the paper bag using the gold pen. When you've finished, place some birdseed or nuts in the paper bag, then tie the bag closed with the twine, leaving a long tail of twine that you can turn into a loop for hanging.

Cut a few holes into the paper bag, then take it outside and hang it on the branch of a tree. Say the following words:

'Persephone, I give to you this offering in return for my wishes coming true. May you manifest what I desire; may you bring to me all that I need for the highest good. So mote it be.'

As time goes by, the paper bag will decompose, leaving food for the birds and wildlife to eat as the cooler weather sets in. The creatures will take your message to the universe to manifest.

Conker protection charm

In the UK and many European countries, autumn sees horse chestnut trees produce an abundance of conkers, which have long been associated with protection and warding off negativity, particularly in Celtic mythology. This charm can be carried out whenever you see a conker.

YOU WILL NEED *a conker.*

If you find a conker in its case while you are out walking, carefully take it home and put it somewhere safe until it naturally cracks open. Keep the conker in your pocket or bag whenever you wish for protection, or place one in your car to shield yourself during travel.

★ Pumpkin pie gratitude spell

Celebrate the harvest and honour the energy of Halloween with this pumpkin pie, giving thanks for all the blessings in your life. Make this pie on or around Halloween to connect with the season's magic.

YOU WILL NEED *425g (15oz) can of pumpkin purée (or the fresh pumpkin flesh from your pumpkin), 400g (14oz) can of condensed milk, 2 large eggs, 1 teaspoon ground cinnamon, ½ teaspoon ground ginger, a pinch of salt, a mixing bowl, a whisk, a ready-made pie crust, a pie dish, a knife and whipped cream for decoration (optional).*

Preheat your oven to 220°C (425°F/gas mark 7). Combine the pumpkin purée, condensed milk, eggs, spices and salt in a bowl and mix together thoroughly with a whisk. Set aside.

Place your ready-made pie crust in the pie dish, then use a knife to carefully carve this symbol of gratitude into the pastry (see reference image on right).

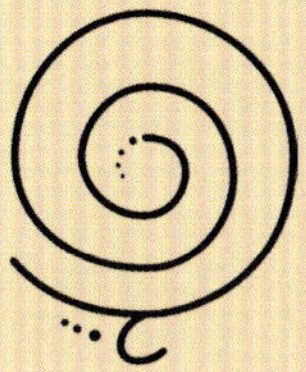

Prebake the pie crust as needed according to the packet instructions, then allow it to cool before adding the pumpkin filling. As you pour the filling into the pie dish, say the following:

'On the eve of All Hallows, I give thanks to Hecate for giving me continuous love, light and blessings.'

Bake your pie for 15 minutes, then reduce the oven temperature to 180°C (350°F/gas mark 4) and continue to bake for another 35–40 minutes.

Allow the pie to cool before topping with whipped cream, if using, then slice and enjoy.

Dream flower divination spell

This gentle flower divination spell helps you receive answers to your questions in your dreams, connecting you to the wisdom of nature during the introspective season. For best results, cast before bed.

YOU WILL NEED *a pen, a small piece of paper, a seasonal flower and a book.*

Write your question on the piece of paper and fold it up as small as possible. Push the paper into the centre of the flower head, then press the flower between the pages of the book. Put the book under or beside your bed. You will dream of the answer to your question.

Pumpkin wish spell

Pumpkins can act as seasonal vessels for your wishes. Perform this spell before midnight on or around Samhain.

YOU WILL NEED *a small pumpkin, a knife, a spoon, a paper towel, soy wax, a heatproof bowl, a saucepan, cinnamon essential oil, orange essential oil, a candle wick, a clothes peg, a few small crystals of your choice, orange ribbon and matches.*

Slice the top off the pumpkin and scoop out all the pumpkin flesh. Dry the inside thoroughly. Melt the soy wax in a heatproof bowl set over a saucepan of simmering water, making sure the bowl doesn't touch the water. Stir occasionally until the wax is fully melted. Allow the wax to cool for five minutes, then add six drops of each essential oil and stir.

Pour the wax into the pumpkin, placing the candle wick in the centre as you do so. You can use a clothes peg to hold the wick in place while the wax sets. Just before the wax fully hardens, place the crystals on top. Once the wax has fully set, remove the clothes peg and tie the ribbon around the pumpkin.

At midnight on Halloween, light your candle and make a wish, then blow it out. Your wish will be granted. You can now use the candle as normal.

Hecate's key ritual

Keys have long been symbols of protection, and they are associated with Hecate, the Greek goddess of witchcraft, crossroads and the unseen. On All Hallows' Eve, harness this symbolism to protect yourself from harmful energy.

YOU WILL NEED *an old key and a length of cord (optional)*

Take an old key (the older, the better) and place it outside your front door for the night. The following morning, bring your key inside and either wear it as a necklace or keep it in your purse to shield yourself from negativity and invite positivity into your life.

Pumpkin enemy banishment spell

The tradition of carving pumpkins at Samhain comes from an older Celtic practice of hollowing out turnips to ward off spirits. These were called Jack-o'-lanterns, after Stingy Jack – a trickster doomed to wander with only a hollowed-out turnip lit by a coal. In America, pumpkins became the lantern of choice as they were native, larger and easier to carve. Ever since, pumpkins have been a symbol of protection. This spell uses pumpkins to banish a harmful person from your life. Cast just before midnight on or around Halloween.

YOU WILL NEED *a pumpkin, a knife, a spoon, a black candle, matches, paper, a black pen, 3 holly leaves and a hammer.*

About half an hour before midnight, prepare your pumpkin for the spell. Cut open the top of the pumpkin and scoop out all the flesh inside. Cut eyes, a nose and a mouth into the pumpkin as you visualize the person you wish to be gone for good. Now place the black candle inside the pumpkin and light it. Take it outside and place it on the ground.

On the paper, writer the name of the person you wish to disappear and the reason why. Wrap the holly leaves up in the paper and twist each end as if you were making a cracker.

At midnight, set fire to one end of the paper and drop it into the pumpkin to burn. Wait until the candle has safely burned down, then take your hammer and smash the pumpkin into small pieces. Walk away from it when you are done.

In the morning, remove the candle case and scatter the pumpkin pieces around outside to feed the birds.

Samhain ancestral love blessing

Samhain, the witch's new year, is the ideal time to call upon ancestors for guidance and blessings. This spell calls on your ancestors to help them guide love into your life and light the path for a soulmate to find you. Cast this spell in the evening on or around Halloween.

YOU WILL NEED *a small pumpkin, a knife, a spoon, a small piece of paper, a pen, a red tealight candle, matches and your favourite incense.*

Cut open the top of the pumpkin and scoop out all the flesh inside. Carve a heart shape into the side of the pumpkin. Write the words 'Love come here' on the paper and place this inside the pumpkin. Place the red tealight candle on top of the piece of paper and light it. Next, light the incense stick and stick it into the top of the pumpkin. Place the pumpkin outside your front door and say the following words:

'I call upon my ancestors to bring forth the love I deserve. I ask that you filter out unsuitable candidates and bring only genuine love to my door. On this special night, may you light the way for my new love to find me.'

Leave the pumpkin outside until the morning, then dispose of it.

All Hallows' exile spell

Halloween is a night when the energies of the living and the departed mingle, creating a powerful moment for cleansing and banishing rituals. It is a potent time to call upon the spirit world to banish negativity from your life. Perform before midnight on or around Halloween.

YOU WILL NEED *a hand mirror, 2 sprigs of bramble, a black candle, matches and a herb bundle (see page 155).*

Place your mirror on the floor, then lay the two bramble sprigs on top of it. Place the black candle behind the mirror. Turn off any artificial light in the room and light the candle.

Sit on the floor in front of the mirror, and lean over it to see your reflection. Say the following words:

'I invoke the spirits of Hecate and Persephone to help me banish (name/situation) from my life now. By the power of three, I call upon you to exile (name/situation). No longer will (they/it) hold anything over me. I bind (name/situation) to the blackest of holes in the universe, and you may now carry the burden of (them/it) for evermore. So be it now. One, two, three!'

Bow your head by way of thanks and allow the candle to safely burn down. Walk away from the spell and allow it to do its work. Mirrors can become portals for allowing spirits into this world, so once the candle has burned away, light your herb bundle and waft its smoke across the mirror. Dispose of the brambles back into nature. Your spell is now cast.

Samhain Tarot spread

Samhain is a sacred time for reflection, messages and wisdom from those who walked before us. This Tarot spread invites their guidance, helping you to see the path ahead. For best results, perform before midnight on Samhain.

YOU WILL NEED *a deck of traditional Tarot cards (such as Rider-Waite-Smith), a white tealight candle and matches.*

Find a quiet space where you won't be disturbed. Light your candle and place it before you. Shuffle your Tarot deck slowly, closing your eyes as you silently invite your ancestors to step forward and share their wisdom. When you feel ready, draw five cards and place them in front of you. The cards represent the following:

1 – Who has come forward – Look for clues in the imagery: a Knight may represent a protective ancestor; the High Priestess a wise matriarch.
2 – What you need to release – The burdens or habits that no longer serve you.
3 – How you can move on – Guidance for healing and progress.
4 – What your new path looks like – The direction the spirits encourage you to take.
5 – What blessings await – Insights into the gifts of the season ahead.

Interpret the cards intuitively; their symbols hold the key. When your reading feels complete, thank your ancestors for their presence, ask them to return peacefully to their realm, and blow out the candle to close the connection.

Samhain shadow-work spell

In this season of shadows, it's important to acknowledge your own. Shadow-work helps you release trapped emotions so you can heal and move forwards. Perform this spell in the evening on or around Samhain.

YOU WILL NEED *a white candle, matches, a notebook, a pen and a fireproof dish.*

Light the candle and stare into the flame for a few minutes to ground yourself. Ask the goddess Hecate to tell you what information you need in order to release your past shadows. This can often be upsetting, because it can bring up all sorts of emotions, but keep at it. If it feels too painful, you may wish to explore what is coming up with a therapist. Write down any thoughts, feelings or emotions that come into your mind. Be prepared to face past challenges. Keep writing until you feel that you have released everything you need to release.

Sit with yourself for a while as you reflect on what you have written down. Now tear the pages you've written out of the notebook and say the following:

'Now is the time to heal. I no longer attach myself to these emotions or feelings. I allow myself to move on with a clean sheet. So mote it be.'

Light the torn-out paper with the flame of the candle, then drop it into the fireproof dish. Leave the candle to safely burn away. When the paper has burned away, take the ash far away from your home.

Samhain cloak-crafting spell

A cloak has long been a symbol of authority and magical ability. Wearing a specially prepared cloak during Samhain can help you step fully into your magical persona, enhancing your focus, intention and presence during your spells.

YOU WILL NEED *a large piece of fabric (such as wool, velvet, cotton or linen) in a colour that feels empowering, fabric scissors, fabric paints or metallic markers, a length of ribbon or cord, sewing thread and a sewing needle.*

Cut a simple rectangular or semicircular piece of fabric large enough to sit comfortably over your shoulders and form your cloak. Decorate it with symbols, runes, celestial designs or any imagery that holds personal significance.

Lay the ribbon or cord at the top of the cloak, making sure a length of it protrudes on either side. Fold the very top of the cloak over the ribbon or cord, then stitch the folded fabric to secure the ribbon or cord in place so that you can fasten your cloak when you wear it.

Once finished, hold the cloak in your hands and say:

'By the power of intention, I bring life to you, to help in my manifestation of spells and protection of myself. So mote it be.'

Your cloak is now blessed and ready to wear when spellcasting. You will notice that your spells manifest quicker when you wear your cloak.

Samhain protection charm

Harness the protective energy of Samhain with a charm you create yourself. For best results, cast on or around Halloween.

YOU WILL NEED *a baking sheet, baking paper, 500g (3½ cups) plain flour, 250g (1¼ cups) table salt, a mixing bowl, 125ml (½ cup) warm water, a rolling pin, seasonal cookie-cutters (such as moons, pumpkins or stars), a straw, acrylic paint or nail varnish in different colours, clear nail varnish and orange and black ribbon.*

Preheat your oven to 150°C (300°F/ gas mark 2) and line a baking sheet with baking paper.

Combine the flour and salt in the mixing bowl and slowly add the warm water. Use your hands to mix the ingredients together until they form a dough. Adjust with more water or flour as needed. Leave to rest for ten minutes, then knead the dough ball for a couple of minutes as you repeat:

'By my hand, this charm shall carry protection and strength.'

Roll out the dough on a floured surface to a thickness of about 5mm (¼in). Take your cookie cutters and cut out shapes, then push the straw through the top of each shape to create a hole. Arrange the shapes on the prepared tray and bake for 1 hour, or leave them on a sunny windowsill until completely dry.

Once cooled, decorate the charms with acrylic paint or nail varnish, then seal with a coat of clear varnish to preserve the design. Thread orange or black ribbon through the holes to complete your talismans. Hang them in a sacred space or carry one with you as a protective charm.

Spirit release spell

Samhain is when the boundary between the living and the departed is at its most fluid, and occasionally, spirits may cross the threshold unintentionally. This spell guides them safely back to the light. Perform it after midnight on Halloween.

YOU WILL NEED *a white tealight candle, matches, a mirror, salt, a herb bundle (see page 155) and a white feather.*

Once you have finished connecting with past loved ones, light your white candle and prop up the mirror behind it, so that the candlelight is reflected in the mirror. Draw a salt circle around yourself and light the herb bundle. Cover yourself with the smoke from the herb bundle and visualize a circle of protection.

Look directly past the candle flame and into the mirror and say:

'This All Hallows' Eve, you were welcome to reconnect with those still on earth. It is now time to retreat back into the light where you belong. You may follow the light back to where is home for you now. So mote it be.'

Blow out the candle and swipe the white feather across the mirror three times. Any spiritual visitors will happily return to where they came from. Clear away the salt after completing the spell.

Samhain closure spell

Samhain is a time to honour endings and prepare for new beginnings, so it's the perfect moment for releasing emotional weight. This ritual uses fire and symbolic layers to help you let go of feelings that no longer serve your growth. For best results, perform at any time on or around Samhain.

YOU WILL NEED *a large onion, a knife, a plate, small pieces of paper, a pen, a white candle, salt, matches and a paper bag.*

Cut the onion in half. Set aside one half for use in another spell or in the kitchen. Trim the base of the other half to make it flat so that it won't fall over on the plate. Loosen the inside layers of the onion with a knife. Take a piece of paper and write down one emotion that you wish to release, such as anger, fear or shame. Repeat with another piece of paper until you run out of negative emotions.

Fold each piece of paper three times, then push it into the onion half, between the layers. Place the onion half on the plate, and push the candle into its centre. Draw a circle of salt around the onion. Light the candle and say the following words:

'On this All Hallows' Eve, I release what does not serve me. I give this all up to make way for a new me. So mote it be.'

Allow the candle to safely burn down, then pour the contents of the plate into a paper bag. Place the paper bag in the trash.

Crow dream-messenger spell

Crows have long been regarded in witchcraft as messengers of the spirit world, carrying wisdom, guidance and insight. In many traditions, crows are associated with prophecy and the liminal spaces between worlds. This spell invites their presence into your dreams so that you may receive guidance or clarity. For best results, cast this spell in the evening before bed.

YOU WILL NEED *a shower or bath, a black pen and a notebook.*

Have a shower or a bath to cleanse your body. When you're all dry and in your pyjamas, take your black pen and draw a crow on either your ankle or your wrist – it doesn't matter whether it's the left or right body part. Say out loud the following words:

***'Crow, oh crow, come to me while I sleep.
Give me guidance and answers that may be deep.
Oh crow, on you I know I can lean,
bring me solutions while I dream.'***

Make your bedroom tidy and cozy so that it feels like a sanctuary. Place your notebook and pen beside the bed and go to sleep. When you wake in the morning, you should have some dreams that you remember, a message that resonates with you or just a feeling that you should be doing something in particular or going to a particular place. Make a note of anything that you remember as soon as you wake up, so that you don't forget.

Apple retribution spell

This spell helps neutralize hostile energy by returning it back to its source. For best results, cast this spell during a waning-moon phase.

YOU WILL NEED *a small piece of paper, a red pen, large apple, an apple corer and a knife.*

Sit quietly and think about the person who has been causing you trouble. Write their name on the piece of paper using the red pen. Use the apple corer to extract the core from the apple. Roll the paper into a small scroll and push it inside the apple. Next, cut the apple core into three equal parts. Discard the middle part and use the two other pieces to insert back into the top and bottom apple, sealing the paper inside. Say the following:

'(Name), your hate will now deteriorate. No longer will you bring harm to me in your words or actions. So mote it be.'

Take the apple to an area of woodland or an open field and leave it there for nature to devour. The paper will decompose.

Banishing bad habits charm

Sometimes, old habits cling to us like shadows. This simple burning spell channels the purifying energy of the waning moon to help banish negative patterns from your life. Cast outside or in a well-ventilated space during a waning-moon phase.

YOU WILL NEED *a pen, paper, matches and a cauldron/fireproof dish.*

Write down the habit you wish to banish and set fire to the paper. Drop it into the cauldron or dish and say:

'On this moon, I burn you away until you are gone from my life. It is now a past memory. So mote it be.'

Let the paper burn safely away. Once the ashes are cool, throw them into the bin to cement the spell.

Release & renew drink

Sometimes the healthiest thing is knowing when to let go of a negative person. This spell helps release your attachment to situations or people that drain your energy.

YOU WILL NEED *3 carrots, 3 beetroots, a vegetable peeler, a blender, ice and a pinch of ground cinnamon.*

Chop and peel the carrots and beets (or substitute them for your favourite veggies or fruit), then add to the blender along with some ice. As you add the pinch of cinnamon, say the following words:

'Surrender, surrender, I do today.
No longer will you ruin my day.
Surrender, surrender, I take my leave.
No longer will I be displeased.
Surrender, surrender, now I'm gone.
No longer will I keep holding on.
So mote it be.'

Place the lid on the blender and blend the ingredients together until smooth. Drink your surrender smoothie in the knowledge that you have now surrendered any hold a situation or person has had on you.

Wicked-tongue silencer spell

Gossip can drain energy and disrupt your peace. This spell creates a barrier against slander so you can maintain your own higher vibration. For best results, cast this spell during a waning-moon phase.

YOU WILL NEED *paper, a black pen and 9 cloves.*

Write the name of the gossip on the paper three times, then place the nine cloves on. Hold your dominant hand over the paper and say:

'Gossip, gossip, off you go,
far away from those you know.
Gossip, gossip, take your words,
your power and your curse.
Gossip, gossip, now be gone.
You have no power from now on.
So mote it be.'

Fold the paper into a parcel to keep the cloves safely inside and keep it somewhere safe for nine days. After this time, you should burn it or bury it away from your home. The person gossiping about you will soon stop. If the gossip persists, repeat the spell, but write the word KARMA across their name each time. This will return their bad energy back to them.

Safe separation charm

Sometimes, people enter our lives for a season and their presence becomes disruptive once their purpose is fulfilled. This spell gently but firmly severs ties with someone who no longer belongs in your life, creating a protective boundary to prevent further contact.

YOU WILL NEED *a clean jar with a lid, gloves, stinging nettles, a garlic clove, a chopped onion, 3 dead leaves and a black pen.*

Begin by blocking and deleting the person's number from your phone and removing them on social media. They need to not have easy access to you. Now take the jar and, wearing gloves, half-fill it with stinging nettles. Say:

'These will sting if you come near me again.'

Add the garlic and say:

'This will deter you from approaching me again.'

Add the chopped onion and say:

'This will form a protective barrier between me and you .'

Finally, write the full name of the person who needs to be banished on the three dead leaves, then add them to the jar. Say:

'The spell is now cast; may you never darken my door again. I send you on your way right now.'

As you say the words 'right now', tightly close the jar's lid. Go outside and bury the jar in the ground, or throw it away in a bin far from your home. You won't hear from this person again.

Graveyard flame release spell

Fallen leaves from a graveyard can be used as conduits for banishing what no longer serves you. This spell combines these leaves with the purifying and transformative power of fire to remove unwanted influences from your life. Cast this spell outside.

YOU WILL NEED *fallen leaves from a graveyard, a pen and matches.*

Gather some leaves from a graveyard and take them home. Write the name of the person you wish to banish on one leaf.

Go outside to an area where there is no risk of fire spreading. Set fire to the leaf and let it drop to the ground. As you do so, say:

'Burn, baby, burn, I remove you. You will not return.'

Keep the other leaves for future use.

Thorned barrier spell

This boundary spell harnesses the natural protective energy of spiny, stingy plants to create a shield around your home. For best results, cast during a waning-moon phase.

YOU WILL NEED *a clean bucket, salt, gloves, secateurs, spiky or stingy plants (such as holly, hawthorn, nettles and roses), a black tealight candle and matches.*

Begin by covering the bottom of the bucket with a layer of salt. Wearing gloves, take your secateurs and forage for thorny or stingy plants, adding them to the bucket. Keep going until the bucket is full.

Place the bucket outside your front door and light the candle. Say the following words:

'Your hexes, your curses have been found.
With this spell they now rebound.
The harm you inflict, the hate you do,
will all bounce back to you.
This is my spell, this is my power,
your ill-will returns at the witching hour.
So mote it be.'

Blow out the candle forcefully to show you mean business and leave the bucket outside your home for 28 days.

Autumn heart release spell

As nature sheds and prepares for change, you are also encouraged to shed what no longer serves you. This spell helps you release lingering emotions from a relationship or friendship and move forward with gratitude. For best results, cast during a new-moon phase.

YOU WILL NEED *a lemon, a knife, salt, pepper, chilli powder, 2 holly leaves and a length of ivy, bindweed or long grass.*

Take some time to think about the person you once loved. Bottling up any emotions, good or bad, will only make them linger. If you get upset, allow yourself to cry.

When you feel ready, cut the lemon in half and scatter a pinch each of salt, pepper and chilli powder on each half of the lemon. Say the following words:

'As the trees shed their leaves, I release what no longer serves me. The time has come for us to say farewell. You taught me lessons I needed to learn, but now we must go our separate ways so that we both can grow.'

Close the lemon halves together and poke the two holly leaves into the lemon's skin. Wind the ivy, bindweed or grass around the lemon to bind the spell. Leave the lemon outside until it rots naturally, then dispose of it in the compost bin.

You will no longer feel remorse at the loss of this other person, but grateful for the memories and ready to move on.

Thistle karma spell

In witchcraft, the thistle, with its prickly nature, is often used to guard against harm and gently warn those who have wronged you. While no actual harm will be inflicted, this quiet hex will silently send a message to someone who has caused you distress without you needing to communicate directly. For best results, cast during a waning-moon phase.

YOU WILL NEED *paper, a pen, 3 milk thistles and matches.*

Write down the full name of the person who has crossed you. Place the thistles in the centre of the paper and roll it up into a scroll while saying the following words:

'(Full name), I strike you with needles, I strike you with prickles, so that you think twice before you harm anyone again. Your time will come, karma will be done, and you will regret your actions – three, two, one.'

Twist the ends of the scroll to keep the thistles inside, then take the scroll outside and light one end, holding it until the paper begins to burn. Throw it on the ground before the flames reach your fingers and stamp on it to extinguish the fire. Now walk away – the spell is cast, and the person will receive their karma very soon.

Justice spell

When someone acts unjustly, it can feel as though karma takes too long to intervene. This spell serves to give justice a gentle nudge. Cast outside or in a well-ventilated space, on a Tuesday, or during a waning-moon phase.

YOU WILL NEED *a red pen, paper, earth from a graveyard, vinegar, beetroot juice, matches and a cauldron or fireproof dish.*

Use the red pen to write down the name of the person who has got away with injustice. Visualize karma as a silver smoke making its way through the air towards them. Place a pinch of the graveyard earth on top of the name, then add three drops each of vinegar and beetroot juice. Mix it all together with your index finger to form a paste that covers the name. Say the following words:

'From today, for your actions you will pay.
From today, you will fail.
From today, karma will be upon your tail.
Look north, east, south, west and over your shoulder,
for justice will prevail to this beholder.
So mote it be.'

Roll the paper into a scroll and set fire to it, then drop it into the dish or cauldron. The spell has been cast, and you can expect to hear good news relating to this matter soon.

Pumpkin hex-blocker spell

This deflection spell uses the protective powers of the pumpkin to shield you from harm. For best results, cast during a waning-moon phase.

YOU WILL NEED *a small pumpkin, a black pen, a white tealight candle, matches and a pinch of sand.*

Place the pumpkin in front of you and draw a pentagram (a five-pointed star within a circle, see page 124) directly on the side of it in black pen. If you know the name of the person who has hexed you, write it underneath the pentagram. Light the tealight candle and carefully place it on top of the pumpkin.

Visualize a white light coming down from the sky and hitting your head, then washing over you like a fountain. Say the following words:

'To the person who is trying to harm me, I am now protected from your bad energy. I have a shield. You can no longer affect me. Your power is useless and is only reflected back to you. So mote it be.'

Take a pinch of sand and sprinkle it on to the candle flame. This should extinguish it. The spell has now been cast. Safely discard the tealight, then leave the pumpkin outside as a feast for wildlife to enjoy.

Deflection stone spell

Just as autumn leaves fall and winds carry them away, this spell reflects any hate or ill-will sent your way back to its source.

YOU WILL NEED *salt, a black pen, a gold pen and a smooth stone.*

Rub salt all over the palms of your hands, then rinse it off. Allow your hands to dry naturally, then use the black pen to draw the evil eye symbol on the palm of your non-dominant hand. Next, take the gold pen and draw gold eyelashes on to the evil eye. This symbolizes your power to deflect negative energy.

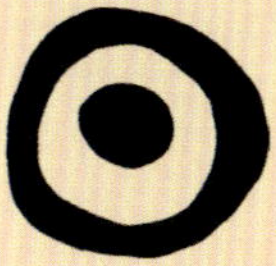

Now rub salt all over your smooth stone, then rinse it and allow it to dry naturally. Once again, draw the evil eye symbol on the stone in black pen, then add gold eyelashes.

Walk towards your front door, holding out your palm with the symbol on it in front of you. Visualize a gold tunnel of protection pushing out from your palm. Open the front door and place the stone outside. Hate will be returned to the person hating on you. You can wash the symbol off your palm whenever you're ready.

New-moon strength spell

Autumn is a season of transformation, when nature lets go of what no longer serves it. You can mirror this process in your own life by releasing whatever weighs you down. For best results, cast this spell during a new-moon phase.

YOU WILL NEED *a carrot, a silver pin, a vegetable peeler, a bowl and a knife.*

Sit quietly with the carrot in your hand. Using the silver pin, engrave all the challenges that you are facing right now directly on to the carrot. Peel the skin from the carrot and place it in the bowl. As you do this, say the following words:

'Vade, Vade! Abi Vade! From this day forth, my challenges will fade. So be it.'

Chop the rest of the carrot into small pieces, then take these and the peelings outside and leave them somewhere where the birds and other animals will find them. They will take away your troubles, leaving you feeling free again.

Lady Justice reversal spell

Most witches understand that energy returns to its source, which is why we rarely seek to curse or hex. However, if someone is acting to harm you or your reputation, you can safely reverse that energy. For best results, cast this spell at midnight.

YOU WILL NEED *the Justice Tarot card.*

At midnight, hold out the Justice Tarot card and call out to Lady Justice, envisioning her scales balancing the situation. Say:

'Lady Justice, intervene and let all harm intended for me return to its source. Let balance be restored.'

Trust that any malicious intentions directed at you will be mirrored back to their origin.

Twilight grounding spell

Twilight – the quiet moments just after sunset – is a powerful time for reflection and connecting to the earth's energy. This spell helps you ground yourself, release stress and restore your inner balance.

YOU WILL NEED *a place outside to walk and a clear quartz crystal.*

Head out for a walk, holding the quartz crystal in your dominant hand. As you walk, inhale and exhale deeply, visualizing the crystal reenergizing your soul. Walk for a minimum of ten minutes. You will feel restored and grounded again.

Karmic mirror spell

Karmic energy is especially potent during the autumn months, when the balance between giving and receiving is highlighted. This spell returns negative actions to their source while nurturing your own heart with self-love. For best results, cast it on a Saturday night.

YOU WILL NEED *a black tealight candle, a small mirror, black peppercorns, pumpkin seeds, matches and rose water.*

Place the tealight candle on top of the mirror, then scatter the peppercorns and pumpkin seeds around the rest of the mirror to completely cover the reflective surface. Light the candle and say:

'(Name), I reflect your karma back to you now. No longer will your power affect me or another. The gods of karma will make sure you receive all you deserve. So mote it be – one, two three!'

On the count of three, blow out the candle flame. Clear away the candle, peppercorn and pumpkin seeds, disposing of them in the bin. Dip your finger into the rose water and draw a heart shape on the mirror. Look into the mirror and say:

'You are loved. It has gone now, and karma will prevail. So mote it be – one, two three.'

Clean the water from the mirror and go on with your evening.

Tulip wish spell

As autumn fades into winter, this spell invites you to reflect on the past season, honour your growth and plant intentions for the coming year. It is a gentle way to prepare for the winter months while keeping an optimistic eye on spring's approach. For best results, cast this spell towards the end of November.

YOU WILL NEED *a white tealight candle, matches, paper, a pen, compost, a flowerpot, tulip bulbs and water.*

Light your candle and sit quietly. On your paper, write down all your achievements from the past 12 months, both big and small, from personal victories to everyday accomplishments. Flip the paper over and write your hopes, intentions and wishes for the coming months. Visualize the person you want to become and the life you want to cultivate.

Place the tealight candle on top of the paper and allow it to burn down safely, sending your intentions into the universe.

Once the candle has burned down, tear the paper into small pieces and mix it gently with the compost in the flowerpot. Plant your tulip bulbs in this enriched soil, tucking them in as you say:

'I honour the lessons of this season. I release what no longer serves me and plant seeds of intention for the future. May these wishes grow and bloom as the earth darkens and awakens. So mote it be.'

Water your bulbs and place them in a sheltered spot. As the bulbs sleep through the winter and begin to sprout in spring, they will symbolize your own growth and the fruition of your intentions.